Retail Survival in Tough Times

RETAIL SURVIVAL IN TOUGH TIMES

2ND EDITION 2023/2024

Are you staying in retail or getting out?

Hymie Zawatzky

NOTE:

This is a guide. It is not a substitute for obtaining legal advice about your lease, finances, or taxation. Nor is it a replacement for a qualified financial advisor. You are encouraged to seek such legal and financial advice where necessary.

DISCLAIMER

At the time of going to press, all information in this book was accurate as the author was able to ascertain within reason. All references to private or state organisations are gratuitous. The author has no financial interest in them and does nor stand to benefit from them in any way

First Published in Australia in 2012 by
Veritax Business Consultants Pty Ltd
16 Eildon Street
Doncaster Vic 3108
Australia

WEBSITE: www.placeofbooks.com

Cover Design by BookPOD
Cover Image by Shutterstock

ISBN: 978-0-6455062-4-2 (pbk), 978-0-6455062-5-9 (ebook)

A catalogue record for this book is available from the National Library of Australia

NATIONAL LIBRARY OF AUSTRALIA

To my wife Joan

Contents

PART 1

MANAGING AND SURVIVING

The State of the Financial and Retail Market

If you are a retailer, you face a number of questions:

Do you think your retail network will survive until Christmas 2023?

With the increases in CPI in Australia now reaching between 8%and 10%.do you have the resources to meet the increases in occupancy costs?

Have you put into place your financial resources with your bank to meet months of traditional slow sales?

If you have a franchise network are you in a position to sustain a decline in retail?

After a successful Christmas in 2022 for most retailers, by 2023 their sales have decreased substantially due to several factors: The banking crisis has affected many retailers with changes in their financial creditability status making it more difficult for those retailers wishing to expand their network. While some retail executives are confident of maintaining or improving profit margins in what is expected to be turbulent times, others expect inflation to put pressure on their profit margins. Hard times are predicted for consumers with anticipated diminished consumption in 2023.

Whilst the labor market is strong at present and the expected increased immigration in 2023 is hoped to boost the labor market, staff demands for increased salaries and wages will put further pressure on store labor costs. Many staff are now simply changing jobs for higher salaries and wages therefore retaining staff will now be one of the top priorities for most retailers.

According to experts, the costs of shipping goods to Australia has increased by over 700%, ordering times have tripled and many retailers are paying earlier for their orders. The result is that the concept of buying goods "just in time" has now disappeared creating a further strain on retail cash resources. As more and more consumers are buying online, the fall in traffic flow to shopping centers has become a problem especially for smaller retailers. They now need smaller retail areas and do not need the costly extra floor space on which they are paying high rentals. Loss of confidence and the collapse of banking worldwide has made consumers nervous in buying goods and services.

Many retailers whose leases have expired at Christmas, are finding it very hard to renogiate with their landlords to reduce CPI increases down from 10% to a more acceptable cap of about 5% or less.

The closure of many bank branches in particular on street fronts is causing many consumers to stay away from small retail complexes which results in a reduction in turnover fror retailers in those areas.

Recent reports indicate that higher interest rates will take a chunk more out of disposable incomes for consumers and increase the proportion of mortgage holders at risk of mortgage distress. The demand for non-essential goods such as clothing and jewellery are expected to deteriorate during 2023 which will greatly affect retailers servicing this area of the market.

Increases in defaults in "pay later" retail schemes could affect sales in 2023 as consumers are may be unable to meet their liabilities.

The CBD retail areas in Melbourne and Sydney are likely to continue to decline as office workers prefer to work at home instead of in their offices in the city. Councils are trying to counter this by trying to attract customers particularly at night, but this is happening very slowly.

CHAPTER 1

Retail Rescue in Turbulent Times

It's tough out there for all retailers. Store closures and downsizing of departments by major department stores have now become the way of retail in Australia. High rents and the rise of online and mobile phone technology is reshaping retail. The reluctance of consumers to buy products other than at the "best or cheapest price" is having a major impact on small and medium retail businesses as well as on many retail chains that have been in business for many years and have survived downturns in the past.

Some retailers unable to adapt to the" new way of retail" have gone into administration or liquidation.

The financial resources of many retail businesses are limited. Any sustained downturn could well result in the failure of your retail business irrespective of whether you are a franchisee or run your own business.

But tough circumstances make people tougher. For this reason, making sound financial decisions has never been more important for you as a retailer, and for the survival of your business. Are you going to leave it to accountants and bankers to measure your performance in the past week or month or are you going to take control?

Yes, you can take control and keep your business healthy and growing, by introducing simple but important steps of key performance measurement indicators. These indicators will take minimal time to implement but they will let you know that your business is still healthy. They will allow you to plan and market for the future and help you to decide on any necessary steps to correct past mistakes earlier rather than later.

There is no quick fix to your problems. The financial survival and health of your business will only be achieved through continuous management and control applied according to a plan backed up by sound knowledge of basic financial issues and changing retail circumstances.

Of course there are still crucial financial matters to discuss with your accountant or solicitor on an annual basis, but the persistent and constant control of the management of your business is up to you. It is you who can keep your business afloat in these uncertain times.

For you to survive in retail and flourish in the current climate, you need to address these vital questions and ask yourself if they apply to your business:

- What can I do about it? Is there an immediate health check that I can apply to my business?

- Is there any action I can take in my store to counter the expanding operations of websites and the growth of ecommerce?
- Does my business look as if it may like close or go into receivership? If so, what are the implications for me and my family?
- If I have too much stock at the start of the year, how do I get this down to acceptable levels by Christmas?
- Given the downturn in the economy, is my rent is too high? If so, how can I negotiate with my landlord for some assistance?
- While negotiating the renewal of my lease during an economic, downturn are there negotiating techniques and concessions I can request that will stand me in good stead when the recession ends?
- If my lease calls for a refurbishment of my business this year, how can I convince the bank to give me a loan?
- How can I prepare and monitor my cash flow statements and take early action ahead of any cash crises?
- Do the ratios in my balance sheet and profit and loss statements give my bank manager, suppliers, landlords or my franchisor confidence to continue supporting me through this difficult time?
- Am I getting the most from my advertising dollar?
- How can I plan to mark down goods to generate extra sales?
- Am I maximizing my profit from each square metre of space in my store?

- If my business looks like it will make a loss, can I reduce costs to keep afloat without wrecking my business completely?

Are you satisfied by your answers to these questions?

If not is there something you can do to improve your situation?

In the following chapters of this book, you will find answers and information that will help you and ensure the continuous health of your business.

CHAPTER 2

Some of the Main Reasons for Business Failures in Australia

There are many reasons given why a business fails. From my experience, I believe that these are among the main causes. Read through this list and see if these points apply to your business:

- Poor planning of the business prior to starting up.
- Not adapting to the new technology of the internet and mobile phones.
- Failure to plan to have a continuous edge over the retail competitors in your category.
- Lack of incentive to monitor the ongoing financial position of the business.
- Not understanding the relationship between the balance sheet and profit and loss statements and how banks use the "ratio and analysis" of these statements to determine whether they will continue to support you.
- Not reacting quickly enough to technical or legislative changes which affect the business.

- Not negotiating adequately with bankers for finance for major capital expenditure required in your business, such as the cost of refurbishing your retail store at the end of a lease.
- Not introducing sufficient security systems within the business to ensure that shrinkage of stock and stealing is kept to a minimum.
- Not having sufficient fixed and working capital in the business
- Not understanding the important relationship between price, volume and costs.
- Poor management of the cash flow of the business.
- Inadequate management of the growth of the business within the parameters of its resources.
- Not negotiating a lease for the premises at a level of rental that is sustainable within the cost structure and sales level of the business.
- Having too much cash tied up in stock on the floor and not enough cash in your till.

Few retailers will be fortunate enough to not have failed in some of these areas. Now is not the time for complaining or blaming others or yourself. It is the time for action. Yes, you can take positive steps to keep your business afloat and to even improve your profits,

An open mind and a willingness to change ways that don't work will take you along that path.

CHAPTER 3

A Management Immediate Review of Your Business

Is your retail business still healthy given the effects of Covid19. Inflation, major increases in lease rentals with COI ranging from 8.0% to 10.0% in some Westfield Shopping Centres in NSW and Queensland and the change in the way consumers purchase their product from retail stores.

Is your business still "an ongoing concern" going forward as certified by your auditors?

Although most retailers prepare a monthly profit and loss account for each store in their group, this does not give management an overview performance of their stores going forward nor the efficiency of the performance of the stores.

To achieve this, we need to measure each store by a set of factors and measurements and as a result we need the following information about each store as set our below:

- Store Name and Number
- Type of store location i.e., Regional, Sub Regional, Neighbourhood or Major Shopping Centre.

- Location either in a regional or metropolitan part of the country.
- Total Occupancy Cot including outgoings and promotion fees
- Area in square meters of each store
- Occupancy cost per square metre.
- Sales for each store for the 12 months to date of this analysis.
- By dividing sales by the area of each store we have sales per square metre.
- We now calculate the percentage total occupancy costs bears to toral sales.
- We require the expiry date of each lease of the stores.
- Total traffic flow to the centres as advised by shopping centre owners from time to time.
- Divide the sales for each store by the traffic flow as advised by landlords to show the sales by visitor of the centre to our store
- We require the name of each landlord for each store.
- We require a list of all competitors of our store in the shopping centre. If none also stipulate this.
- We require the number of staff in each store together with their total working hours per annum
- By dividing total store sales by number of hours worked per annum we will have the sales per hour for that store.
- Calculate the percentage of total wages to sales.

From the above information and using an excel spread sheet set up the base document information and total each column.

Regional vs Metropolitan Stores Analysis

- Our first sort will show us the total sales for regional versus metropolitan stores.
- The sort will also give us the sales per visitor for metro vs regional stores.
- The sort will also give us the gross rent per square metre of metro vs regional stores.
- The sort will also give us the sales per square metre of metro vs regional stores.
- The sort will give us the percentage occupancy to sales of metro vs regional stores.

Although the sales and profitability of country stores is not as high as metropolitan stores and shopping centres, this is offset by much lower costs of rent and staff costs. Country stores also attract customers from small cities often 50 kilometres from our store. However, we have the cost of freight of getting our products to country stores, Freight costs have also increased substantially with high inflation.

Country areas are often more stable than city areas and customers tend to shop in the store where they may know the staff and do not rely on online buying which is an additional cost of delivery for metropolitan shops.

During Covid many city dwellers moved to the country areas which boosted country store sales without substantially increasing the cost of rent. However, post Covid a number of returned to their metropolitan homes.

Sales per square metre and rent per square metre are much lower than in metropolitan stores and shopping centres. Also, percentage occupancy to sales is also much lower.

Retailers should in my view continue to have a medium percentage of their stores in country area, however the costs of climate change have had a major impact on country areas and locations in small towns is essential.

Climate change and the floods and fires which have hit rural areas of Australia is also a vital consideration in opening a country store.

CHAPTER 4

With the Current Upheaval in Retail and Having Done the Management Review as Set Out Above, Is the Business Still Healthy or Do You Need a Doctor?

Below is a checklist of questions with explanations which clearly outline the risk that your business faces if these answers are not adequately addressed.

Read this checklist carefully and you will find it provides you with an idea of the areas in which your business needs the most attention. It will prove to be an extremely important document as it pinpoints key problem areas. Remember to take this list with you when you visit your accountant.

The business health checklist to be answered by every small business owner

Question 1:

Have you given any personal guarantees during the year? If so, were they blanket guarantees, or did you put only certain personal assets at risk?

Risk

In the event of a default all your personal assets could be taken.

Question 2:

Does your business structure protect your personal or family assets? Are you a company, a family trust, or a private personal operator?

Risk

Different structures have different levels of personal liability, and each must be viewed individually.

Question 3:

Are you maintaining adequate liability insurance in the event of a claim or a cyberattack"?

Risk

If you are held negligent, you (as the business owner) can be held liable regardless of your company structure.

Question 4:

Are you depositing all your income? Are your records in sufficient order to sustain a GST audit?

Risk

The tax office can and will fine you and would even try to take possession of your personal assets.

Question 5:

If you are in a partnership, do you have a current buy-sell agreement in place in the event of the death or disability of one of the partners?

Risk

Forced liquidation of the business could result from the absence of such an agreement.

Question 6:

If you have a family business, have all parties agreed in writing to their responsibilities and understand what this means?

Risk

Disharmony in a family and business can result in poor business practice and inadequate management decisions.

Question 7:

Have you given adequate attention to the issues of retirement and superannuation planning and possibly the issue of business succession?

Risk

Everyone is subject to old age and ill health. Creditors will be more at ease if the business has a succession plan in place and long-term debt is assured f repayment.

Question 8:

Are all directors' loans adequately documented representing an arms length transaction?

Risk

Debit balances on directors' loans may be classified by the tax office as dividends.

Question 9:

In the event of your lease expiring, have you ensured that you will have sufficient funds to both meet the cost of refitting your shop and the cost of paying for possible large rental increases?

Risk

Major rental increases or substantial capital costs for refitting of premises can put pressure on cash flow and business profitability.

Question 10:

Have you conducted a full stock check recently? Does your business appear to have much stock shrinkage?

Risk

Stock shrinkage reduces gross profit and can have a major impact on cash flow

Question 11:

Is the technology in your business such as point of sale equipment, internet access to your products and website in line with the latest available equipment?

Risk

Your inability to obtain instant information and analysis of your sales or the inability of customers to contact you from outside your premises could quickly result in loss of sales

Some quick action tips if you said "no" to any of the previous eleven questions:

Guarantees

If you are asked to give a personal guarantee on a lease for your premises, as is usual in any leasing transaction, always try to put a cap on your exposure.

For example, insert a clause in the guaranteed document, limiting the personal guarantee to possibly three months rental. This should then be sufficient time for a landlord to re-let the premises.

If you run your business as a company, the Australian Corporations law allows companies to function with one director. Even if you or your wife and children are the owners or shareholders in the business, only appoint one of the family as the director. This will shield other members of the family from having to give personal or director's guarantees.

Business Structure

If you have more than one small business, and for example you own two pharmacies, it is important to have each business as a separate legal entity. This will prevent creditors in one business trying to attach the assets in the other business for the payment of any outstanding debts.

If you have a registered trade, brand or product name, by which your business is known, and for which you have spent considerable amounts of advertising dollars to be instantly recognised by the public, it is good sense to have that trade name registered in a shelf company or trust.

This entity should be separate from your normal business, with no assets or liabilities other than that name. Then if you go broke in that company, you will still own the trade name and in time you will be able to start up again.

You will find answers and action plans to other problem areas in your business throughout the book.

CHAPTER 5

Taking On the Growth of Internet Online Shopping and Mobile Phone Technology

In your retail store

One of today's biggest challenges for retailers is the rise of internet and mobile phone online buying.

Consumers have now realised that for many years they may have paid too much for their goods. The rise of online buying has shown them that by surfing the net they can buy the same branded product overseas for very much less than in Australian stores, even with the added cost of postage.

The consumer doesn't even have to leave the comfort of his homes to do this. He has an amazingly wide range of products to choose from, far more than you could ever stock in your store. And with a click of a button, he can buy.

Now the absurd position exists where instead of hunting for bargains on the Boxing Day Sales, consumers can now access the internet and buy massively discounted branded products on the

Thanksgiving and Black Friday sales in the USA. These sales take place at the end of November and even with a week or two for delivery, the goods can be in Sydney or Melbourne well before Christmas. Once again local retailers miss out.

The bottom line is that retailers cannot take Aussie consumers for granted and assume that their buying trends of the past will continue. They have to adapt to the new retail environment.

Well then let's now look at this new trend and see what we can do to turn it to our advantage

The impact of internet shopping on shopping centres and retailers

In the case of large shopping centres, many small retailers and chains who rely on the traffic flow generated by the anchor tenants like department stores are feeling the pinch. And the department stores themselves are starting to feel pressured by the growth of internet and mobile phone shopping.

Without a strong department store to draw traffic flow, landlords of these centres, are now focussing on reinventing speciality stores from whom they receive the majority of their rental income. Some commentators have even suggested that this shift in demand will eventually result in shopping centres looking more like theme parks than traditional shopping centres.

Since the recent downturn, consumers have become more cautious and concerned about saving as much as possible for that rainy day. This change in attitude means that "easy go shopping" and putting a string of retail purchases on credit is a thing of the past. Today's consumer is more likely to spend cautiously, check prices carefully on the internet, buy on eftpos instead of on their credit card and even put money away in the bank . Higher bills for electricity, bus fares, have also contributed to this state of mind of the consumer.

So how can retailers turn this new form of consummer spending to its advantage

More and more people are using the internet and social media. The language of buying has changed and lately people respond as they do on Facebook. They have become used to pressing "like" "share" or "comment" buttons to make their opinions known. As it is the customer who calls the tune, you the retailer will have to keep up with these new trends. Let's now look at how we can take advantage of these new trends in buying goods:

- Create a website of your store with online capabilities and with your products and prices clearly displayed on the website. This will turn your store into a giant catalogue.

- Ideally every retail business should have the following online essential software.

- A website that you can update yourself.

- An email newsletter that you can post to subscribers through the internet.

- A blog that you can connect to your website and to your Facebook fan page.

- A good idea is to offer loyalty programs discounts or coupons on your site to prevent your customer checking prices with his mobile phone and buying from your competitor.

- You should make certain that you focus on finely targeted individual sales instead of mass sales.

- It is essential that you ensure that your supply chain logistics and inventory management are perfect. You dare not run out of stock.

- Remember that unlike overseas internet sites, you will still have to pay GST, so price your products accordingly.

- Be certain that your security measures on mobile phone transactions are of the highest quality as customers continue to be concerned about the security of their transactions.

- Do your utmost to create something innovative with the presentation of your product. Ikea for instance, allows the IPhone to select a piece of furniture from the catalogue and using the phone's camera, place it anywhere in the room and then change its size to fit the perspective.

- A large fashion store in the UK allows the customer to select a garment, hold it up to her body and then look in a mirror. The fashion garment is then imposed on the image in the mirror to show how the dress fits on the customer. All this without having to go into the store's change room.

- It is essential that staff training is orientated to customer needs. Staff must know their products. In addition, the techniques of add-on selling and closing the sale before the customer goes elsewhere, are vital.

- You should encourage every customer to contribute to and be part of your monthly email newsletter.

- It is a good idea to form alliances with other complimentary retailers and showcase each other. Create your own collective VIP card between you and promote each other in your newsletters. These days retailers need to stick together and networking is an excellent means of survival.

If you adopt these measures, you will give your customers not only a rewarding channel to buy products, but it will encourage their loyalty to your store. Even more importantly, it will give retailers the opportunity to talk to their customers in real time.

There will always be those customers who want to see and feel what they are buying. Many people still want and need the help and advice of a salesperson when buying. Online buying on the internet and the use of mobile smartphones will not end conventional retailing as there is still place for bricks and mortar but online buying will reshape the consumer experience.

CHAPTER 6

Special Key Performance Indicators for Retailers to Test the Viability of Their Business

To keep your business healthy, especially in tough times, you need to keep a sharp eye on its performance.

The two best performance measurement criteria that should be used by speciality small business retail operators in tough times are:

- A. The measurement of the businesses stock turn
- B. Break Even Analysis

A. Stock turn over

What do we mean by stock turnover?

Stock turnover is defined as the number of times during a specific period, usually one year, that the stock on hand is sold.

At a time such as the present, slow stock turn means that your cash flow is not being turned into money to pay your creditors. The stock is simply lying on the shelves. If this is allowed to continue too long, it is a recipe for quick bankruptcy.

In addition to building up your cash flow, a high level of stock turnover in a business has several advantages for any retailer: Remember your store has a limited amount of space.

It must always be your objective to get the most profit per square foot out of your valuable space. Slow movers tie up valuable space.

Some Advantages of high stock turns are as follows:

- Merchandise on the shelves is always fresh.
- Losses due to changes in technology are reduced.
- Costs associated with maintaining stock, such as interest, insurance, and breakage are all reduced.
- You are able to take advantage of discounts offered by suppliers.

The formula for calculating your stock turn

Most retailers who keep computerized records of their merchandise at cost price use this cost price method of calculation.

Take the cost of goods sold during the year and divide them by the average cost of your stock on hand

$$\text{Stock turn} = \frac{\text{Cost of goods sold during the year}}{\text{Average stock on hand (at cost)}}$$

You will find this information is readily available from your trading account and the calculation is easy to do.

More often end of year stock figures are used for this calculation (instead of averages) but there are advantages to using averages of the stock holding at both the start and the end of the year. Levelling out high and low stock levels held during peaks or slow months will give you the yearly average.

> **TIP:** As different businesses have different levels of stock turn, you should always try to ensure that you are in line with other retailers selling similar products.
>
> It would be useless to compare your stock turn with that of a fashion store or hardware store if you own a camera store.

So how can you as a small retailer maximise the stock turn in the business?

If you are not achieving the average turnover that is applicable for your industry or would like to improve your stock turnover, these are some useful ideas that you could adopt:-

- Identify your best selling items promptly.
- Eliminate, if possible, slow selling items.
- Reduce your range so that you ensure your optimum range contains your strongest and most profitable product groups.
- Maintenance of a minimal stock of "have to keep lines".
- Buy in an efficient and timely manner.
- Only do business with reliable distributors.
- Allocate prime selling positions to your best selling classifications.

B. Break even sales

What does the term break even sales mean?

Break even sales is defined by accountants as "that level of sales at which the gross profit on sales will recover the total expenses of the store." Over that level, the net profit of the store will be equal to the gross profit on such excess sales. This means that at the break-even level of sales, you have made sufficient gross profit from trading, to cover all the expenses of your store, such as rent and salaries for that month or period.

One of the most important calculations that every retailer should make each month, is to determine the break-even sales of the store. In the current difficult climate, this is even more essential than usual. Once you have established your break-even figure, it is very easy to make an estimate of your profit or loss for the month without having to wait for your accountant to do the calculation.

This is how you calculate your break-even sales:

Your costs for the month are divided into variable expenses and fixed expenses.

Variable expenses are those which vary directly with turnover for instance salaries and wages. In reality, most monthly expenses that you will have are *fixed expenses*, apart from a few casual staff wages.

For the purpose of this break-even analysis technique, the total expenses for the month can be considered as fixed costs.

Formula for break even sales

$$\text{Break even sales} = \frac{\text{Total fixed costs}}{\text{Gross profit}}$$

Example:

Let us assume that you, a retailer, have a gross profit margin of, say, 34% on sales over a number of years and that your budgeted expenses for the month of June was $21150

$$\begin{aligned}\text{Break even sales} \atop \text{for month} &= \frac{\text{Total expenses}}{\text{\% Gross Margin}} \times \frac{100}{1}\end{aligned}$$

$$= \frac{21,150}{0.34} \times \frac{100}{1}$$

$$= \ \$62,205 \text{ for month}$$

This means that at a level of sales of $62,205 you will make a gross profit of

$62,205 × 34%	$21,150
Less Total Expenses for month	$21,150
Net Profit	Nil

According to the above definition, all sales greater than $62,205 for the month multiplied by your gross margin will give you your net profit for the month.

If you went to your accountant with the same level of expenses of $21150, the gross profit that you usually achieve of 34% as above, together with a sales figure for the month of $100000, (which was actually made for the monthi achieved), your accountant will present you with a profit and loss account which looks like this:

Sales	$100,000
Gross Profit (34% of $100,000) =	$34,000
Less Expenses	$21,150
Net Profit for month	$12,850

You don't need to wait for your accountant; you can make your own simple calculation in the following manner:

Sales for month	$100,000
Less Break Even Sales	$62,205
Difference	$37,795
Net profit for month = $37,795 × 34 %	= $12,850

When your accountant does meet with you, he will simply verify your calculation.

This formula is also useful when you need to calculate the extra sales your business will have to make in order to pay for an additional expense. Have a look at the following helpful examples

Example 1

Your store manager suggests an advertising campaign in the local newspaper to boost sales. The campaign would cost in the region of $10000

If you divide $10000 by 34% (the same gross percentage as previously) you will need the following amount of extra sales to pay for it:

$$\frac{10000}{0.34}$$

$$= \ \$ 29,412 \text{ extra sales}$$

If the proposed expense does not look like achieving more than $29412 worth of extra sales, then you should decide not to go ahead with the advertising campaign.

If you reduce each extra cost to the *amount of sales* that you need to recover it, everyone working in your store will understand the formula.

In addition, if you evaluate every additional expense in this way, you will be able to determine the extra sales you will require to pay for any new expense that comes up.

Though this seems like a very rigid test and may not always be practical, at a time of cost containment, when sales are falling, it is likely to be your best approach.

Example 2

If the sales in your store are falling and you have to let go a staff member earning approximately $25000 per annum, the following calculation will be useful.

You divide $25000 by your gross profit of 34% = $73530

This will allow your sales to fall by $73530 per annum as a set off for reducing the staff member earning $25000 per annum.

Example 3

You are paying a rental of $100000 per annum and you have a 5% automatic rental increase of $5000 on the anniversary date of the lease. On the day your rental goes up, you can calculate the amount your future sales will have to increase, to offset the rental increase as follows:

$5000 divided by your gross profit percentage of 34% or $14705 per annum to cover this rental increase

However in a tough retail climate, where sales may be falling due to increased competition, or due to rising on-line purchases, it may not be possible to increase your sales. You may even have to ask the landlord to waive the rental increase for that year.

We will look at waiving rental increases in later chapters of this book.

CHAPTER 7

Benchmarking Your Business

A key method of ensuring that your overall trading performance is and remains competitive, is by benchmarking your businesses (also known as KPI's) against retail industry sector comparisons and standards.

Utilisation of the information gained from this will allow you to identify the productivity and efficiency of your retail business and provide you with guidelines for achieving improvement.

Variations between any individual results, best practice and the overall industry sector standards, can be adjusted by putting into place a corrective action plan.

A financial benchmarking analysis and report

This type of report would generally cover the following questions about:

Profitability

What gross and net margins should your business be able to achieve?

Return on investment.

Is your business providing an adequate return on the money invested?

Business risk

What is the gross break-even figure that your business is required to achieve? on a weekly/monthly or yearly basis?

What drop in revenue could your business absorb before incurring losses?

Efficiency

Is the level of expenses too high relative to businesses of a similar size?

How efficient are the costs of your business?

Productivity

Are your staff generating enough revenue for each dollar of labour spent?

Is your business generating adequate income per square metre of floor space?

Stock control

What level of stock are businesses like yours holding to achieve a similar level of sales?

What stock turn level is required to ensure maximum stock control?

Is your business generating an adequate gross margin return on inventory?

Example:

Let us look at the Benchmarking Analysis for say footwear retailers last produced by an EBC Business Benchmarking for larger stores in shopping centres, together with some recent performance benchmarks produced by the Australian Taxation office

Understanding the analysis in this business will help you to apply the principles used to your own business. You will also gain a better understanding of benchmarking as a technique.

The following points emerged from the analysis:

- Personnel productivity and stock management are the two critical areas in footwear retail.
- High personnel productivity keeps a major cost, namely wages, under control.
- Stock management is critical. Having this year's fashion in stock is vital. Not being left at the end of the season with sizes that are large or too small is essential.

The most profitable shoe businesses in their survey showed the following.

- Stores were larger
- They had a much higher personnel productivity. This showed that staff were working effectively converting sales into enquiries and "up selling"
- Stores had a better stock productivity.

- Stores had higher stock turn coupled with higher gross profit margin.
- Stores generated more revenue from each dollar of assets.
- Owners of stores worked more hours per year.

CHAPTER 8

Margins, Markups and Markdowns

Confusion can lead to bankruptcy without you, the business owner knowing it.

The failure to fully understand and utilize the important business concepts of margins, mark ups and mark downs and the part they play in managing a retail business, can damage your business and even result in its collapse without you realising it

Ask yourself if you are you in control of these three vital concepts or if they are slipping from your grasp. Let's examine them carefully:

1. What are mark ups?

A Mark Up is the *difference* between the *cost price* and *selling price* of an item and it is expressed as a *percentage of cost price*:

It is calculated as follows:

$$\text{Mark up} = \frac{\text{Selling price} - \text{Cost Price}}{\text{Cost price}} \times 100$$

Example: If we buy a handbag for $60 and decide to sell it for $ 90

Then according to the formula:-

$$\text{Mark up} = \frac{\$90 - \$60}{\$60} \times 100$$

$$= \frac{30 \times 100}{60}$$

$$= 50.0\,\%$$

2. What do we mean by margins

The margin is the *difference* between the *cost price* and the *selling price* and is expressed as a *percentage of selling price.*

It is calculated as follows:

$$\text{Margin} = \frac{\text{Selling price} - \text{Cost Price}}{\text{Selling price}} \times 100$$

Thus in our example of the handbag:

$$\text{Margin} = \frac{\$90 - \$60}{\$90} \times 100$$

$$= \frac{30 \times 100}{90}$$

$$= 33.33\,\%$$

It is important to note that though there is a complimentary relationship between mark ups and margins, the margin is always the smaller of the two figures.

When we talk about the gross profit you are making, we are actually talking about the margin you are making on the sale. In reality, these two terms; *gross profit and margin, are one and the same.*

Given that you know the desired mark up, there is a quick table that can be used to compare the margin with the gross profit made on a product.

% Mark up on cost of product	% Gross Profit on margin on Sales Price
10.00	9.0
11.1	10.0
20.0	16.7
25.0	20.0
33.3	25.0
50.0	33.3
66.7	40.0
75.0	42.8
90.0	47.3
100.0	50.0

The mark up you decide to use depends on your particular approach to pricing and your type of business. Some businesses tend to have high mark-ups and low turnover, whilst others tend to have low mark-ups and a high turnover.

3. What do we mean by markdowns

A Mark Down is defined as the *difference* between the *original selling* price and the *new selling* price. It is expressed as a *percentage* of that original selling price.

Example:

An item sells for $90 and after three months you decide to mark down its selling price to $70:

$$Mark\ down\ =\ \frac{\$90 - \$70}{\$90} \times 100$$

$$=\ \frac{20 \times 100}{90}$$

$$=\ 22.2\ \%$$

There are occasions during a year, particularly in the current economic climate, when money is tight and people have become very price conscious. They may be comparing your price for the product. If your product is discounted to meet the online price, then they will tend to buy from you.

In this situation you may be marking down your stock either to clear slow-moving merchandise or stimulate sales. Whilst markdowns are likely to stimulate extra sales, if the increase in sales is insufficient, not only will your overall profitability be affected but the expected gross profit of your business will fall.

It is important to bear in mind that sales and price reductions go hand in glove. Be sure that you know the exact impact of price cutting on your profitability.

The following table is a guide to help you calculate the increased sales you will need to make in order to compensate for various price reductions.

Percentage increases in sales necessary to break even after a price cut

Price	Present Gross Profit Margin (%)							
Cut	10	20	30	40	50	60	70	80
5%	100	33.3	20.0	14.3	11.1	9.1	7.7	6.7
10%		100.0	50.0	33.3	25.0	20.0	16.7	14.3
15%		300.0	100.0	60.0	42.9	33.3	27.3	23.1
20%			200.0	100.0	66.7	50.0	40.0	33.3
25%			500.0	166.7	100.0	71.4	55.6	45.5
30%				300.0	150.0	100.0	75.0	60.0
35%				700.0	233.3	140.0	100.0	77.8
40%					400.0	200.0	133.3	100.0
50%						400.0	250.0	166.7

Example:

If you normally sell a pair of boots for $100 that cost you $60, you usually make a profit of $40 and a gross profit percentage to sales of 40 %.

Assume you normally sell 50 pairs of boots per year, and then you will make a gross profit on those boots for the year of:

$$50 \times \$40 = \$2000$$

If you decide to mark down the shoes by 20 % for a sale i.e. you propose to sell the boots for $80.

If you follow the table you will find that if the gross margin is 40%. If you want to cut the price by 20%, the increase in sales necessary to break even after the price cut is 100.0%.

Thus, in order to still maintain your total Gross Profit dollars on that line of boots you will have to increase your sales by 100 %

Normal quantity sold	50	Sales quantity required	100
Normal Profit per pair	$40	Sale Profit per pair	$20
Normal Gross Profit Dollars earned	$2000	Sale Gross Profit Dollars earned	$2000

4. Budgeting for and monitoring markdowns

In the current economic climate in retailing today, markdowns are a fact of life. Whether we like it or not, despite the buying of merchandise becoming more sophisticated, is still subject to buyer error.

So how do we measure the performance of our buyers?

Changing fashions and colours, or ordering too much of a particular product, can result in markdowns being required in order to sell your merchandise. If you accept this as a fact, you can now set up a budget to monitor markdowns to determine just how effective your buying has been.

Obviously if your markdowns are greater than you thought, this will have a major impact on your profits. If they are lower than you thought, you will see the effect on the bottom line profit.

Setting the budget will be of no value unless, at the same time, you set up a method of estimating the value of proposed markdowns from your normal prices. This is simpler to do than it looks.

You will find that there are many available computer programs to do this for you. But if you prefer to operate a calculator manually and use an analysis book, it can do the job just as well.

5. Preparing a mark-down budget

In order to set up your budget for markdowns for next season, you need the following accounting information.

1. The projected monthly sales for your store, or if applicable by department.
2. Your mark-up on products that will allow you to calculate your "1st margin on sales." This refers to the gross profit on sales if all goods were sold at full margin.

3. The final gross profit you expect to show in your accounts after markdown.

The following example demonstrates an accounting budget and a markdown budget

ACCOUNTING BUDGET

	$	%
Sales Budget – Net	1000	100
Cost of Sales	600	60
Gross Profit	400	40

MARKDOWN BUDGET

Mark up on Goods	100%
Gross Profit at Full Margin	50%

It is important to remember that the cost of sales will remain unchanged irrespective of whether you are having markdowns or not.

For example, if all goods were sold at the full mark-up of 100 % on cost, you would have achieved theoretical sales for the year of:

600 + 100% of $600 = $1200

Therefore you can make the following calculation

$$\begin{array}{l} \% \text{ Mark-downs} \\ \text{for the year} \end{array} = \frac{\text{Theoretical Sales} - \text{Actual Sales}}{\text{Theoretical Sales}} \times 100$$

$$= \frac{(\$1200 - \$1000)}{1200} \times 100$$

$$= \frac{200}{1200} \times 100$$

$$= 16.67\%$$

The above example shows that you are budgeting for markdowns with a sales value of $200 for the year. Having a mark down budget figure provides you with access to further valuable information.

If you multiply the selling price of a product with the number of products sold during the year, you will be able to calculate the actual value of your markdowns. This is a valuable figure for your budgeting.

If you compare the actual value with your budgeted value of markdowns, you will then be able to measure the efficiency of the buying department and their ability to obtain the margins on products that the company expects to achieve.

It makes sound business sense to ensure that you have a markdown budget as soon as possible

Using the Same Financial Ratios as Your Bank to Take the Temperature of Your Business

You will find that in difficult times, the only way your bank manager will continue to give you an overdraft and other borrowing facilities, is if you comply with his set of ratios and analysis of your accounts. In this way you will be able to convince him that you will be able to repay the money lent to you.

Your balance sheet and profit income statement represent a complete financial record of your business. Together with the other financial information you gather on a weekly or monthly basis, you can develop a set of measurements that will independently allow you to monitor both your current position and your progress. Armed with this information, you will be in the driver's seat when you come to face a similar analysis by your bank.

You can develop this invaluable set of business measurements through a series of financial relationships or ratios.

What do we mean by ratios?

A *ratio* is nothing more than one number in relation to another. For example, the relationship of 2 to 1. Or the relationship can be expressed as a percentage, such as gross profit of 35% of turnover.

What is the value of ratios for a retailer?

The importance of the ratio is its ability to measure and manage your financial effectiveness. Without it you will be operating by guesswork.

Reading the ratio thermometer

Financial ratios in isolation have little significance. They only have significance when comparisons are made with past or future ratios, or comparisons with competitors, industry standards or a comparison with "rule of thumb" standards. This comparison provides the window for you to see into your business and develop ways to improve its operation.

Especially in tough times like these, financial ratios can tell you about the stress and strains that are at work in your business. They mesh together like the gears in your motorcar, to propel your business forward. Not knowing your ratios is a little like the first time you attempt to drive a manual car – a bumpy ride at best....

One necessary set of ratios that we use is known as the Key Performance Ratios. They assist us in analyzing the liquidity, the profitability and efficiency of the business. In tough business times, these ratios are particularly important, especially to bankers, in assessing your overdraft facilities or in the granting of an additional bank loan.

Caring for your business

In line with the theme of treating your business like you would care for the health of your own body, ratio analysis is equivalent to taking the temperature of the business.

Ratio Analysis is an excellent method for determining the overall financial condition of a small business and its ability of surviving the current retail crises. It puts information from your financial statement into perspective and it helps you to spot financial patterns that may threaten the health of your business.

Even though management accounting is often clouded in mystique, you can analyse and interpret financial statements yourself. And one of the most widely practiced ways is by the use of financial ratios.

Make a diagnosis to assess which ratio will perform best for you

The question that each small business person needs to establish is *"which relationship to measure."*

The different ratios and how to calculate them

First decide on the questions you want to ask about the performance of your business. Then look at the various means of calculating this by using one of the simple ratios. Once you decide on the type of ratio your business needs the rest is straightforward.

To do this you need sufficient information to get the job done without it becoming confusing.

> **TIP:** Remember that no individual ratio tells the entire story. Taken together however, ratios allow you to begin the process of analysing your business performance and even more important, planning for the future.

In general, ratios can be used to analyse your business by:

- Comparing the current performance to prior years – giving you the business trends
- Comparing your present performance to other retailers in your field
- Comparing your ratios with your budget or plans so that you can develop a working strategy for the future.

The link between the two financial statements

One component that measures the functioning of the business and its health through the inter-relationship of the balance sheet and income statement is *efficiency.*

Efficiency is the technique of converting assets (like stock) to revenue, converting revenue to profits and structuring liabilities and net worth so that you can use borrowed money as well as your own, to finance your business.

Your bank manager probably applies all the ratios indicated below when he examines your financial records

TYPES OF RATIOS

What are the steps you need to take to analyse your business?

Gather together all the accurate financial information available in the business for the past two or three years if available.

- Set out these statements on a spread sheet format side by side.
- Now you are ready to use that same spread sheet to calculate the ratios.

Your bank manager probably applies all the following ratios when he examines your financial records:

BALANCE SHEET RATIOS

There are two balance sheet ratios that you need to know about– current ratios and quick ratios.

Current ratio

This ratio measures not only the solvency of your business but also your business' ability to pay short-term debts. This is done by comparing the current assets and current liabilities of your business.

It is particularly important if you are thinking of borrowing money from your bank or obtaining substantial credit from a supplier.

Changes in your current ratio over a number of years could be indicating financial problems on the horizon. The key is to find out why the ratio has changed.

How to calculate a current ratio:

$$\frac{\text{Current Assets (Stock + Debtors +Cash)}}{\text{Current Liabilities (trade creditors + short term borrowings + overdraft)}}$$

How does this particular ratio measure the health of your business in dollars and cents?

It is the "rule of thumb" ratio used by bankers to measure the solvency of your business. The current ratio should be expressed to be approximately 2 to 1. (That is to say your total current assets are twice your current liabilities). Businesses with growing sales and a short operating cycle in turning over their stock, can work well with a lower ratio than 2 to 1.

However, given the unpredictability of the selling cycle of retailing, particularly in the current climate, you should not allow yourself to be held to these terms by bankers, as you may not be able to pay your suppliers or take advantage of discounts for cash.

What does this ratio mean – in terms of your business' own performance and industry standards?

If it is too high: This may indicate an imbalance in your investment in long term assets or it can show an economic situation developing, which is conducive to maintaining high liquidity. If you have a high cash balance you should take advantage of a major price decrease. On the other hand, it could show an overstocked warehouse, since formal stock is being taken into account.

If it is too low: This may indicate that you're financing long term assets with short-term money.

Quick ratio

This ratio (sometimes known as the "acid test" ratio) measures the liquidity of the business – your ability to raise cash quickly if pressed by suppliers. It is similar to the current ratio but the difference is that stock is not taken into account. Stock doesn't always sell quickly and including it in such a calculation could distort the figures.

Potential creditors like to use a quick ratio instead of the current ratio because it reveals the business' ability to pay off trade debt under the worst possible conditions, such as at a time of recession.

How to calculate a quick ratio

$$\frac{\text{Cash} + \text{accounts receivable}}{\text{Current Liabilities}}$$

What this means in dollars and cents:

This ratio may be used by a supplier, in a situation where the business places an abnormally high order or when the supplier has in the past not been paid on time. Most suppliers know that on a quick sale, stock only achieves 20% -30 % of its value. Hence the need for this ratio.

The rule of thumb for the quick ratio is 1 to 1. However this rule of thumb needs to be interpreted with care, particularly for retailers who operate on cash or credit cards with stock as their major asset.

How do you interpret this ratio in terms of your business' performance and industry standards?

If it's too high: This may indicate an excess of cash. Normally it implies an under-investment in stock and it shows up in reduced sales and reduced profits. This occurs because you don't have enough stock to sell and your customers go elsewhere.

If it's too low: It may manifest itself in a shortage of cash. It usually indicates financing of long-term assets with short-term money or problems associated with an over investment in stock.

INCOME STATEMENT RATIOS

Profitability ratios

Every retailer wants to know if the business is profitable. Therefore, calculating the key ratios pertaining to your profit and loss account, is a critical piece of information available to you.

The absolute level of profit may provide an indication of the size of your business, but on its own it says very little about the performance of your business.

In order to evaluate your level of profit, your profit must be compared and related to other aspects of your business.

Profitability ratios will inevitability reflect the business environment of the time.

Again, comparisons with other businesses in the same industry segment will provide an indication of management's relative ability to perform in the same business and economic environment.

Profitability ratios consist of two types:

1. The first is profitability compared with sales, which shows how well each dollar of your sales generates profit.
2. The second is profitability compared with assets. This determines how hard your assets are working to generate profit.

1. The gross margin ratio

This ratio measures the profitability of the business at the gross profit level.

For example a gross margin of 35% means that for every $1 of sales the business produces 35 cents gross profit.

Some business owners will use the anticipated gross profit to help them price their products or services. Whilst some factors, like competition and demand, play a part in pricing decisions, a gross profit measurement is a good starting point in product pricing.

How to calculate a gross margin ratio

$$\frac{\text{Gross profit}}{\text{Sales}}$$

What does this ratio mean if compared to your business' own performance and industry standards?

If it is too high: This means the business is earning its full mark-up without resorting to discounting in order to clear stock. However, a policy of not discounting could result in a very much slower stock turn with out-of-date stock still sitting on shelves.

If it is too low: This should be of concern to you. A low gross margin usually represents a reduction in sale prices. This reduction may occur through markdowns or an increase in cost of sales that may not have been passed on to customers by shrinkage, not taking discounts due to excessive stock or low cash. It may even be caused by matching prices with a competitor and trying to gain market share at a price.

2. The net margin ratio

This ratio represents the average net profit earned by each dollar of your sales.

It represents the operating profit of the business. Or it can be seen as the amount left from your sales dollar after deducting your cost of goods sold (that is your gross profit) and your ordinary operating cost of doing business.

Your operating percentage simply tells you the percentage of your sales that will turn into profit. Again, reductions in this percentage might indicate the need to re-evaluate your pricing, your suppliers or you need to look for other ways of cutting down on your operating costs.

How to calculate the net margin ratio

$$\frac{\text{Net Profit before Tax}}{\text{Sales}}$$

What does this ratio mean when you compare it to your business' own performance and industry standards?

If it is too high: This means the business has been able to contain its overheads, like salaries, wages and occupancy costs which are fixed costs, irrespective of the level of sales.

If it is too low: This is of serious concern as it shows that expenses that have risen substantially during the year have not been offset by the necessary increases in sales. To survive you will have to address expenses very carefully, particularly labour and occupancy costs.

3. The occupancy cost ratio

This ratio measures the occupancy cost of your business. It determines the amount of rent your business can afford to pay.

A rule of thumb is that the percentage should be no greater than 30% of the gross profit of the business, that is a business with a gross profit to sales of 40% cannot afford to pay more than 12% (that is 30% of 40%) by way of occupancy cost.

How to calculate the occupancy cost ratio

$$\frac{\text{Total rent} + \text{all outgoings} + \text{promotion or marketing levy}}{\text{Sales}}$$

What does this ratio mean when you compare it to your business' own performance and industry standards?

If the percentage is too high: This means that your business can't afford the rental and that you would have to seriously consider seeking premises in a lower cost area. This could lead to your loss of goodwill built up because of your trading in that location for a number of years.

If the percentage is too low: You probably signed a lease at the bottom of the leasing cost cycle and now the landlord will be looking to a substantial increase in rental at the earliest opportunity.

4. The return on assets ratio

This ratio is used to reflect the profit earning performance of your firm's assets.

It measures the efficiency of the total assets of your business in generating net profit.

It is important to note that a retailer's fit out cost has to be amortised over the term of the lease, which is usually 5 years. Sufficient profit must be generated to amortise the asset as well or it will have very little value at the end of the lease.

How to calculate the return on assets ratio:

$$\frac{\text{Net Profit Pre Tax}}{\text{Total Assets}}$$

What does this ratio mean when you compare it to your business' own performance and industry standards?

If percentage is too low: A decline in the return on investment will occur if expenses rise faster than sales revenue. Therefore this ratio should always be examined in conjunction with the gross and net profit margins. A decline may also occur if the asset base increases at a faster rate than the net profit. If you find this happening it could mean a decline in stock turn.

5. The stock turnover ratio

This ratio measures the rate at which stock is being used on an annual basis.

For example, a stock turnover of 6, means that the average dollar volume of stock is used up almost 6 times during a financial year. It may also mean that you are turning over your stock and earning profits on that very stock every 2 months.

How to calculate the stock turnover ratio:

$$\frac{\text{Cost of goods sold}}{\text{Stock at year end}}$$

What does this ratio mean when you compare it to your business' own performance and industry standards?

If it is too high: This may show that you have too little stock on hand to risk taking up special buys.

If it is too low: This may indicate excessive stock holding. It is necessary you always have fresh stock on hand, or your regular customers may turn away from your store.

Stock turn days

This ratio converts the stock turnover ratio calculated above into an average stock on hand figure. For example, a stock turn day figure of 60 days means that your business keeps an average of 60 days of stock on hand during the year.

How to calculate the number of stock turn days

$$\frac{365}{\text{Stock turnover times}}$$

What does this ratio mean when you compare it to your business' own performance and industry standards?

If it is too high: This may indicate inadequate stock on hand or lack of risk to take up special buys.

If it is too low: This may indicate excessive stock holding. If this is the situation your goods may go out of fashion quickly or you may not have enough fresh stock on hand and your regular customers may go elsewhere.

The following example illustrates how to use the last two ratios and at the same time compare your performance with industry standards.

Example:

If your sales for the year are $1200000 and your cost of sales are $840000, your store makes a gross profit of $360000. Given your closing stock of $140000, then the calculation is expressed as follows:

Sales	1,200,000
Cost of sales	840,000
Gross Profit	360,000
Closing Stock	140,000

Stock turn as per the formula is thus

$$\frac{840,000}{140,000} = 6 \text{ turns}$$

Assume the industry standard for your retail category is 6.8 times

$$\text{Your Business} = \frac{365}{6 \text{ stock turns}} = 60 \text{ days}$$

$$\text{Industry} = \frac{365}{6.8 \text{ stock turns}} = 54 \text{ days}$$

Does 6 days make such a difference to your business? Well, let's convert those days to dollars to find out using simple mathematics

Since: $$\frac{\text{Cost of Goods Sold}}{\text{Stock on hand}} = \text{Stock turnover}$$

Then: $$\frac{\text{Cost of Goods Sold}}{\text{Stock turnover}} = \text{Stock on hand}$$

And: $$\frac{\text{Cost of Goods Sold}}{\text{Target stock turn}} = \text{Target Stock}$$

In this case, if the industry standard is 6.8 times and your business was in line with the industry, using the above formula you will have the following:

$$\frac{\text{Cost of Goods Sold}}{\text{Target stock turn}} = \text{Target stock}$$

$$\frac{840{,}000}{6.8 \text{ times}} = 123{,}500 \text{ target stock on hand}$$

This calculation tells you that you are holding $16,500 too much stock ($140,000- $123,500). If you divide this by the 6 days difference, as calculated above, it tells you that one day of stock turn is worth $2,750 in cash flow. If the stock had not been sitting there it would be turned into cash.

Ask yourself if your banker, who has the industry standards available, would be willing to lend money to subsidise your inefficiency? I don't think so particularly in difficult times.

Once you have decided which ratio or ratios will contribute to your business, consider the following:

Package up the information so you can see relationships.

- Calculate the financial ratios;
- Record you industry benchmarks if available;
- Compare your results with industry benchmarks;
- Analyse if possible the cause of the problems;
- Take action by formulating a plan, implementing it and monitoring the results.

The importance of the working capital cycle

It is worthwhile noting that a second business cycle is also used by many bankers in Australia in assessing the health of the business. This is known as the working capital cycle that operates within the balance sheet.

This cycle measures the relationship between cash, inventory and accounts receivable, and the speed and efficiency in which accounts receivable and inventory can be turned back into cash.

Most retailers do not have outstanding debtors as they mostly work on credit or debit cards but the principle remains the same.

Managing the cycle more efficiently is critical for the owner of the business and the faster the circle turns, the more cash it will generate, the lower the bank loans that will be needed to supplement the working capital of the business.

Bankers often refer to this cycle as "the survival cycle". They need to know what sucks cash out of this cycle to pay for such items as fixed asset replacements.

Remember that long-term assets should be financed by long term liabilities. Using working capital which is an asset that turns over within every 12 months should not be used to pay for new fixed assets.

CHAPTER 10

Owning the Property in Which You Operate Your Business and Making It Work for You in Tough Times

The rent that you pay determines the value of the property to a landlord. This rent is then capitalised by a valuer at a percentage. It then becomes the yield that an investor would expect to receive from that property.

The yields range from 6% for a large shopping centre to 13% for smaller properties, depending on their location.

Example:

The property that you own and from which you trade has a capitalisation value of 10%. If you pay yourself a notional $50,000 per annum in rent then the value of the property is expressed in the following equation

$$\frac{\$50,000}{10\%}$$

(This is how property valuers and property owners would express this equation)

$$= \quad \$50,000$$

Against such a valuation, a bank may be willing to advance you 75% by way of a mortgage. You would then be in a situation to borrow $75% of $500,000 or $375,000 and acquire another property or invest the funds in your business.

You now have a valuable asset that you can underpin by entering into a lease between yourself and an entity owning the property. You are now in a position where you can raise extra capital if you desire.

If your business can afford it you can raise the rental you can afford to pay and by so doing increase the capital value of the business. This is a method of using the lease effectively to improve the value of your family assets.

CHAPTER 11

The System of Open to Buy to Control Your Buying and Managing Your Stock Levels

Let us view the following situation

1. After the Christmas sales you find that you have not made the expected and hoped for turnover.
2. You find that you are overstocked, that discounting has not had the desired effect and that you need to place new orders.

What do you do?

Having too much stock at the start of the year and not being able to move it is a problem many retailers face at present.

A useful technique to help a retailer solve this problem is the introduction of an *"open to buy system"* whereby you can control your buying, particularly for some key departments in your business

Why do you need an open to buy system in your business?

- Open to Buy systems have been used by major retailers throughout Australia for many years to:

  ◊ control their buying.
  ◊ ensure that investments in stock do not exceed their budgeted holding amounts.

- The overbuying of stock can result in the need for markdowns to reduce stock to manageable levels at the end of a season. However, this can have a drastic effect on the profitability of a business.

Can this management technique work for your business?

You may ask yourself why you need this technique, if your relationship with your supplier is so good that you can simply phone through an order and it is delivered to you immediately? Pharmacists are in this position with most suppliers.

So why should you change?

The reason is quite simple. As more and more new departments are introduced into retail businesses like pharmacies, we find that non-traditional suppliers to retailers require orders to be placed a number of months in advance. Some examples of these include, in the case of pharmacies, health shoes vitamins and gifts for Christmas. In addition, orders for products for the coughs and colds area, which are seasonable in nature, also have to be placed well in advance.

When retailers in toy shops or fashion retailers plan their trips to Sydney, Melbourne and other major cities for their industry fairs, to make their major purchases for the year, one of the most critical decisions is how much can they or should spend?

Therefore, when you make these important decisions, it is necessary to ensure the following:

- that purchases are made from suppliers in good time
- that the purchases are within the cash flow of your business

A proper open to buy system will give you the control that you need.

It is critical to the profitability of the retailer to work within these limits and thus avoid the fatal end of season markdowns.

Remember that every time you buy merchandise at an industry fair, there is pressure from industry representatives for you to buy even more. If you buy more than you can sell, even if you order the right items, where will you get the money to pay your bills?

The answer is proper purchases planning and to have an open-to-buy plan which will ensure that markdowns do not happen.

The plan will ensure that the flow of merchandise into your store will be correct to support anticipated sales at the desired stock turn rates and give you a positive cash flow.

Traditional inventory control or accounting systems will not provide you with this important projected information, yet it is one of the most effective cash flow and stock management systems available to you.

It is not hard to set up an open to buy plan. Retailers familiar with the use of a simple personal computer and spread sheet will be able to prepare one very easily.

How to achieve your planned objectives?

To achieve your objectives, it is critical for your purchases to be planned in light of the following: -

* bearing in mind your current stock levels at the start of the season.
* looking at the level of stock you wish to have on hand at the end of the season.
* looking at the budgeted levels of sales you need per month.
* looking at the number of times you turn over our stock in a season.
* being aware of the number of purchases you have committed yourself to at any point of time.

All the above ingredients are added into your.....

OPEN TO BUY PLAN

How then does this plan operate?

The whole objective of the plan is to enforce a discipline on the retailer that only allows future purchases to come in at the end of the season, if they are in line with the PLANNED CLOSING LEVEL OF STOCK that was set at the start of the season.

This plan is obviously not set in concrete and will change as the season progresses.

For example, if sales achievements are exceeding budgets in a particular month, the open to buy plan during the balance of the season would have to be increased, otherwise stocks would be deleted and sales targets in later months will not be achieved.

Remember that the intention of this plan is for the closing stock to remain unchanged.

Do you keep your open to buy plan at cost or at retail?

Some retailers maintain their open to buy plans at retail others prefer to keep them at cost. Both have advantages and disadvantages. I would recommend that as it is simple that you keep it at cost.

Keeping the plan at cost

For simplicity purposes, most retailers maintain their stocks and purchase orders at cost. All you need to do to maintain the open to buy at cost is to reduce *budgeted sales* to *cost of sales* by applying the *budgeted gross profit*.

So before we continue with the steps necessary to formulate the open to buy plan, let us look at an example of the sales budget for the next six months and apply this calculation to reduce it to cost.

Calculation to reduce cost of sales

From your sales budgets, calculate what our cost of sales will be in each month and enter these in the cost of sales line for the season

If sales is 100% (A) and the Gross Profit is anticipate to be 40% (B)

Then Cost of Sales will be A - B = 60%

Let's look at our sales budget for 2022/23 and apply the above formula

SALES BUDGET

SUMMER 2022/23

	Budget Sales 100%	Gross Profit 40%	Cost of Sales 60%
Sept	2167	867	1300
Oct	1833	733	1100
Nov	1917	767	1150
Dec	2833	1133	1700
Jan	1167	467	700
Feb	917	367	550

Formula for calculating an open to buy plan

The formula for calculating your open to buy on your spread sheet will always be as follows:

Closing stock budget at cost
+ sales budget for month at cost
– opening stock at cost
– goods on order due in the month at cost
= Open to Buy for the Month at Cost

Example:

This example shows more clearly how the plan works. You will understand more about using a spread sheet for your calculations by looking at the annexure at the end of this section of the book on page?

Month of September

Closing stock Budget at 30 September	2250
Plus: Sales Budget at cost	1300
	3550
Less : Opening stock at 1 September at cost	1000
	2550
Less : Goods on order due in September at cost	2400
Open to Buy At Cost	150

Continuing with the previous example, if for instance your budgeted sales at cost for October are $1100 and November $1150. On the basis of a two month stock holding, it is then prudent to ensure that you have stock on hand by the end of September of $2250.

Some questions often asked by retailers about open to buy programs are as follows:

How long in advance should an open to buy program be calculated?

It should be calculated some months prior to use, particularly where seasonable buying takes place as in the Christmas season where buying of gifts starts early.

It is always wise to have your open to buy programme in place before you go to the trade fair.

Should I always buy to the full amount of my open to buy?

From a strategic perspective, it is advisable *not* to buy to the full value of your open to buy plan. Rather allow yourself a percentage of about 10 % to take advantage of special deals or purchases of new items. You can even replace stock that sells out quicker than anticipated.

How do I go about setting the stock levels that I wish to hold at month ends and at the end of the season?

This is determined by the normal annual stock turn of your business. Assume you have a stock-turn of six times a year based on your previous results. This means that you are turning your stock over every two months.

It is essential to have on hand or in transit, stock to at least the next two months cost of sales value, or you could run out of your stock and you could loose out on sales.

An example using your spreadsheet

Now using your spread sheet let's put all the information together and set up an open to buy plan.

Remember that this is merely a guide and that you will have to add changing and seasonal factors such as Christmas sales and spot sales in your calculations.

Step 1

You have made the decision that you wish to end the season at the end of February with the same level of stock as the opening stock at beginning of September, namely 1000

Using your spread sheet enter 1000 as your opening stock in September 2022 and 1000 as your closing stock at the end of February 2023. *This closing stock figure cannot change.*

Step 2

Now let's look at the on-order line and put in each month the goods you have already ordered from suppliers as well as forward charging and possibly proposed orders from the fair.

The figures in this example are as follows

Sept	2400
Oct	1800
Nov	850
Dec	600
Jan	500
Feb	450

Now fill this in under the appropriate month on the spread sheet

Step 3

From your previous calculation now inset the cost of sales for each month.

Step 4

On the basis that you turn your stock over six times per annum, it will be necessary to regard the next two months cost of sales as the closing stock. Thus, as seen previously, because you propose a cost of sales of $1100 in October and $1150 in November, your budgeted stock at the end of September should be $2250.

Enter this figure and complete the remainder of the row on your spread sheet.

Step 5

With the exemption of the closing stock at the end of February 2022, which is fixed, you can complete the closing month's stock levels in the spread sheet for all the intervening months.

Step 6

- Using the formula you can now complete the missing figures in September - namely opening stock of $1000 plus on order of $2400 giving you a sub total of $3400 available for sale during the month.
- From this sub-total you can deduct the cost of sales for the month of 1300 to give you a sub-total of $2100 (your theoretical stock on hand).
- However, you have calculated that to meet the next two months sales, your stock on hand should have been $2250.
- Therefore you now deduct this budgeted stock from your sub- total. When you look at your new sub-total, you will find that your targeted stock is short by $150 to meet your targeted stock level.

You thus have open to buy of $150.

If your purchases for the month of September are increased to:

$2400 + $150 = $2550, then your actual stock at the end of the September will equal your theoretical stock. This is then the stock you need to hold in order to meet the cost of the next two months sales.

Step 7

The budgeted closing stock of $2250 at the end of September now becomes the opening stock at the beginning of October and so on.

You can now re-arrange the formula provided that you have placed no further orders prior to the fair, and that you propose to order all your stock at the fair. Or that you intend to create a purchasing budget to link to your proposed cost of sales.

The formula is now as follows:

> Purchases for month = Closing stock + cost of sales – opening stock

You can now place your purchase orders in the exact month required to achieve the sales levels that you have budgeted for and finish up with the level of stock that you planned for.

It goes without saying that the level of purchases will depend on the level of sales that are achieved in your store during the season.

If your trend of sales decreases, do not be afraid to cancel orders to keep your buying in line. If you do not, you will not achieve the level of stock that you have set yourself to close with at the end of the season.

In this way, at the end of each month you will be able to amend the spread sheet with your actual stock on hand and with new projected sales figures. This provides you with a revised open to buy. It may mean that you may have to cancel orders or bring orders forward, but at least *you will have a plan and you will know what to do.*

There is nothing worse than attempting to estimate your stock needs by pure gut feeling.

I can recommend this plan to all retailers who have had problems in the past with ordering. This programme works best when the entire retail team is involved in buying for the store and are committed to the plan and the discipline that it requires. You will feel the benefits of using it very quickly.

CHAPTER 12

Requesting and Negotiating a Rental Rebate from a Landlord in Difficult Trading Conditions

As the economic recession deepens, simply to survive, more and more retailers are in desperate need of some rental relief from their landlords. I am firmly of the belief that retailers should never be afraid to ask for a rental abatement. You will find that landlords do not wish to loose a good tenant particularly in the current retail climate.

The task is often left to the retailer to start the negotiations by preparing a letter asking for rent relief and requesting a meeting with the landlord. A typical letter requesting a rebate from a landlord would be along the following lines:

The Landlord
ABC Shopping Centre
Dear Sir

Re Lease of XYZ Pty Ltd at the   Shopping Centre

As you are aware retail trading conditions in Australia have deteriorated substantially since the start of this financial year, with most retailers

91

experiencing lower sales and reduced margins. Our category of retail sales is no exception.

Our performance at the above centre has now reached a level where our Board of Directors has requested me to seek some form of rental abatement from you, to assist us in the short term, until retail conditions improve at the centre.

We are thus proposing the following for your consideration:

1. That we be provided with a rental abatement of $xxxx per month either by way of a credit on our rental statement or by way of an advertising concession. This abatement is to be for a period of 6 months to 31 December 2023 when it can be reviewed.

2. We will continue to pay our share of outgoings and marketing levy as per the lease.

3. Any rental increases as per the lease due prior to the will be waived and forgiven.

Looking forward to a favourable response to the above request.

Yours faithfully

If you receive an outright "no" from the landlord, you may have a substantial problem. If you have been well in arrears with your rent payments or not paying your rent on time, the landlord may not be concerned should you leave the centre.

If the landlord has agreed to meet with you to discuss the situation you need to prepare your case very carefully as you are likely to have only one go at explaining why you need rent relief.

Putting up your case

1. You need to have all the necessary information with you at the meeting to justify the rent reduction and be willing to share it with the landlord.

2. Have your accountant prepare a current, accurate set of financials.

3. If you are in a shopping centre, ascertain the number of retailers in your category when you started the lease and the current number.

4. Ascertain if possible the impact of online sales in your category and how this is affecting your business.

5. From statistical data available, determine the trend of traffic flow to the centre for the last few years, and whether this has been in decline or not.

6. Demonstrate that you have tried to execute all alternative strategies to improve sustainability.

7. Show that you have a plan of action as to how you will leverage the possible rent relief. For example, a local advertising campaign to bring more customers to your store and to the centre.

8. If your rent is currently in arrears show how you propose to pay it back.

9. It is important to make the landlord feel that you are both in partnership in the business and that both need to share the risk in the current climate.

10. No one knows how long the retail downturn will continue so ask for your rent relief in say 6 monthly periods with the situation to be reviewed at the end of each period.

11. Be creative in how the rent relief is paid to you. For example, it may be more tax effective or more valuable for the landlord to give you an advertising allowance in lieu of rent relief, which in addition to such allowance being tax deductible, also maintains the rental income for valuation purposes.

If you are planning to renegotiate a new lease, I would recommend you to my book "The Retailers Handbook Post Covid 19"

CHAPTER 13

A Proposed New Lease Offer on the Renewal of Your Lease During 2023

The following is a suggestion of what should be included by retailers in their lease offers or renewal of a lease during a retailers during this difficult retail situation that we are likely to suffer during 2023

This letter has been prepared for a pharmacy tenant but can be adapted for any retailer depending on the circumstances of negotiation.

Project Leasing Manager
Happiness Shopping Centre
P.O. Box
Melbourne
Victoria

Dear Sir/Madam

Re: Lease XYZ RETAIL STORE – Shop 12 - Happiness Shopping Centre

Thank you for your letter of invitation of 10 July 2023. We have now visited the centre and have reviewed the indicative plan which you have presented us with.

As such we would be willing to put the following proposal for consideration. to our board.

PROPOSAL

Location: Shop 1 Lower Ground Floor

Lessee: Partners as per current pharmacy practice as of this date or a management company to be nominated.

Size: 200 square meters (subject to survey) Irrespective of the surveyed size of the Premises, the rental in year one will not be more than the agreed amount.

Handover Date: Approximately 4 October 2023

Lease Term: 5 Years and 3 months commencing 28 days after handover of the premises or commencement of trading from the store whichever is the later in a clean shell state condition. We require the extra three months to allow us to trade through an additional Christmas.

Option Period: 2 terms of 3 years each

No restrictions will be accepted on the lessor exercising such option.

Base rent: $xxxxx for year 1 plus

However, we will only pay 75% of the base rental until the following has been completed by the lessor.

- All stores are open and trading.
- All car parks are open and available for customers
- All the lessor's works have been completed.
- The supermarket is open and trading.

Rent Reviews: CPI. for the term of the lease. Such CPI increase will be no greater than 5% in any one year during the lease or option period.

Unless the parties have agreed to a new rental, a market review will be conducted on the exercise of the option in accordance with the Retail Tenancy Act.

During the option period rent will again increase at the rate of CPI annually from the start of the second year of such an option period.

Outgoings: As Applicable to our tenancy (exclusive of carbon tax).

Promotion Levy: 3% of base rental.

Opening Promotion: $1000 payable 14 days prior to commencement of trading.

Guarantor: The directors of the Company.

Bank Guarantee: The equivalent of 2 months base rental excluding GST.

Percentage Rental: Pharmacists are legally required not to share their income with anyone who is not a pharmacist. Therefore, percentage rent will not be applicable in the lease.

However, for planning purposes the lessee will undertake to provide, monthly sales figures comprising front of shop sales plus NHS income.

Legal Costs: Each party will be expected to bear its own legal costs in respect of the lease preparation, or any ancillary documents or guarantees. The lessee will be responsible for the costs of registering the Lease.

The Act applicable to lease: The current Retail Leases Act in the applicable state.

Exclusivity: A special provision is required as follows; that no more than one tenancy will be permitted to dispense pharmaceutical products (as provided for under the National Health Scheme) at the centre during the lease term and option period.

In the event of the redevelopment of the centre of more than 100 retail tenancies allowing for an additional pharmacy being permitted in the centre, then the lessee shall be entitled to the last right of refusal on the lease for such tenancy.

OR

If no exclusivity has been promised, in the event of a second pharmacy opening in the centre, our rental will be permanently reduced to 75% of the rental payable at that time.

Payments: All rental, outgoings, and promotion contributions to be payable monthly by way of EFT only. No direct debits will be acceptable.

Lessor Contribution: $xxxxx contribution is payable 7 days after presentation of Invoice (including GST).

Repayment of the contribution in the event of assignment of the lease will be as per your lease offer. However, if the approved assignee is prepared to accept the liability then no repayment will be required by the pharmacist.

Fit-out: We will supply our normal set of plans/ drawings for approval at no cost prior to proceeding with the shop fit- out.

Signage package will be provided for approval.

Consulting, design, survey costs or other engineering costs will be payable by the lessee will be capped at $X.

There will be no charge for hoardings.

Kiosks: Whilst we accept kiosks as part of a centre layout, no kiosks will be erected within 10 meters of our lease line which will affect the sightline of the premises.

Rent in Advance: The one month's rental to be paid on the signing of the lease which will be applied to the first month's rent when payable.

Pub Liab. Insurance: $20m

Retail Category Classification: Pharmacy

Permitted use: The operation of a pharmacy and health food shop including retail sales and services and the operation of a mini lab, as well as other goods and services as normally undertaken by a pharmacist as determined from time to time, (such as sales of confectionary, sporting and disability aids, health shoes, wheelchairs as well as the operation of a beauty parlour or perfumery)..

The premises will also be used from time to time for the operation of medical and para-medical service providers, and special medicine preparations.

Solicitor: This offer would naturally be subject to our solicitor sighting and approving the disclosure statement and lease and its terms.

Lessors Works: The premises will have sprinklers and air conditioned o a quality in accordance with the Australian air conditioning standard. The landlord shall guarantee that the premises shall be water and weather sealed at the time of entering the lease.

Lease Terms: All amendments to standard leases previously negotiated to be carried forward to the lease for this centre.

Painting: We will undertake to paint and restore the store not at fixed intervals, but as and when necessary by mutual agreement during the lease term.

Electricity: In the event of electricity been charged to us as a result of bulk buying by the lessor, the tariff charged to us will be the "best tariff" rate applicable and in accordance with current electricity regulations. The pharmacist will be able to use its own electricity provider if it is more cost effective.

Binding Agreement: There will be no binding agreement between lessor and the lessee to enter into a lease, until the necessary legal documentation is drawn up and executed by all parties.

Storeroom: In the event of a storeroom being supplied, as part of the agreement, we require a licence agreement be supplied for such storeroom to run concurrently with the lease and to terminate at the same time as the lease. No outgoings will be applicable for the storeroom.

Outposts: The landlord shall permit us to have two outposts per annum in the centre mall at the commercial rate. The timing of such outposts shall be by mutual agreement.

Relocation: Relocation of our pharmacy during the lease or option terms as a result of the total re-development of the centre, will be permitted once the heath commission has approved such relocation and the landlord agrees to compensate us and pay for all costs of relocation, erection and fit out of such new pharmacy as provided under the Act.

Deregulation: In the event of the deregulation of the pharmacy industry, allowing supermarkets and other retail chains to incorporate pharmacies within their stores, the lessee shall be permitted to either surrender the lease or renegotiate at the time the terms and conditions of the balance of the lease with the lessor.

Should the above proposal be acceptable to the lessor, we would be happy to submit an amended formal lease invitation to our board of directors for approval.

The document will need to be signed and dated.

Some additional terms that could be included in lease offers

Quite often the parties believe that they have agreed to the commercial terms of the lease but then find that when they receive the landlord's standard lease documents there are terms and conditions contained therein which are simply not acceptable to the retailer.

To overcome this, retailers have started to put the following special conditions in their lease offers. In any event, when checking the lease, you should request that such clauses be deleted or amended. (Some of these provisions have already been dealt with previously).

Kiosks: No Kiosk (other than existing Kiosks) will be permitted within 10 meters of our lease line which will affect the view of our store or impair ingress or egress from our store.

Directors Guarantees: If the retail store is a company no director's a guarantee or bank guarantees will be provided by the lessee.

Method of Payment of Rent: The payment of rent and outgoings will be. by electronic transfer and not by direct debit.

Opening Promotion Levy: If the tenancy is to be in a new shopping centre and there is to be a "once off" opening promotion levy, this levy must be payable 14 days before the commencement of trading from the store. In addition, the lessor will provide details within 3 months of opening on how the opening promotion contributions have been spent.

Consulting Fees: The retailer will not be responsible for the payment of any consulting, plan approval or engineering costs in respect of the fit out.

CPI Rent Increases: If rent increases are to be based on CPI plus a fixed percentage which is permitted in all states except Victoria, we require a provision that if CPI is negative that rent will fall on the anniversary date of the lease.

Outgoings: If we do a deal based on net rent plus outgoings and the deal is say for less than 1 year (which in some states would take us outside the Act), irrespective of whether we fall under the Act we must make the following lease provision:

- In the case of stores in Queensland, South Australia and Victoria, land tax is not recoverable as an outgoing from tenants.

- In the case of West Australia management fees are not recoverable as an outgoing from tenants.
- In the case of Victoria management fees may not increase by more than CPI annually

Tenancies in Strip Centres: If the retailer is opening a retail store in a strip centre that may be subject to flooding from storms, we must provide that the lease contains a condition requiring the landlord to agree that on the handover of the premises to the tenant that the premises are water and weather sealed.

Insurance: The following provisions should be included:

- Public liability insurance will be taken out to an amount of $20m and in addition the retailer will only keep an industrial special risks policy.
- The company's insurance policies are to be in the name of the retailer and the lessor's interest only will be noted in the policy.
- No policy will be taken out by the lessee in respect of limitation of the landlord's liability in the event of a claim.

Fit Out Contributions: If you have negotiated an incentive deal with the landlord who may have contributed to the fit-out, the following provision in the lease is required; that the fittings making up the contribution will remain the property of the landlord for the term of the lease but the retailer may or may not remove them at the end of the lease term. The taxation implications of this type of incentive are overly complicated and you should first clear this with your tax adviser.

In the case of a fit-out contribution which includes a "claw back" provision, there must be a provision in the lease stating that in the event of a relocation to an assignee acceptable to the lessor, no repayment of the fit-out contribution will be required by the tenant retailer provided that the assignee is prepared to accept this contingent liability.

Cost of Hoardings during Fit-Out: All costs of hoardings during the fit-out store will be payable by the lessor.

Painting and Restoration during the lease term: Painting and restoring of the premises during the lease term and option periods will occur as and when necessary, by mutual consent and not as decided by the landlord unilaterally.

Quality of Air Conditioning to be provided: You must request a provision in the lease to ensure that *"The lessor shall provide air conditioning to the premises of a quality so as to provide comfort conditions even when the lighting heat intensity exceeds 50 watts per square metre of the floor area of the demised premises including other heat producing equipment within the premises".* This is in accordance with the Australian standard.

Fire walls sprinklers and emergency lighting: We require a provision in the lease or confirmation from the landlord that irrespective of these costs being included in the definition of outgoings in the lease, that the landlord agrees to ensure the following:

- That the landlord will conducts a six-monthly inspection of the fire walls, and these will be tagged to this effect.
- That the landlord will conduct a 3 monthly inspection to check that the pressure to the sprinklers in your tenancy is correct and that they will function in the event of an emergency.
- All fire hydrants hoses and reels within the common area of the centre are also checked at least every 3 months

to ensure than the equipment has not been vandalised and will work in an emergency.

Change of signs and colour: We require a general provision that no permission will be required from the lessor in the event of a total change of corporate colour or image change of the entire network.

Restoration of shopfront during lease term: There should be provision in the lease that this will only be required not at fixed intervals but as and when necessary if mutually agreed to by both parties.

Services: In the event of electricity or gas being provided by the lessor to the premises, this will be charged at the same tariff rate as paid by the landlord or at the best rate. In addition, the retailer will be able to acquire such services from their own providers.

Relocation: A section of the lease offer must include the following:

- That the alternative premises offered will be in a position in the centre which in no worse than the position the lessee currently enjoys.

- The rental will be the same rental as the current lease adjusted to take into account the commercial value of the new premises at the time of relocation as agreed by the parties, or in the absence of agreement, as determined by a valuer appointed by the Small Business Commissioner (in the case of Victoria)

- The lessor will in addition, agree to waive the "making good" and decommissioning costs of the existing premises and pay for any surrender of lease legal costs.

Market Reviews in Victoria: In Victoria, if there is to be market review on an exercise of the option in the lease; ensure that there is a provision in the lease for the market review to be completed first before you must exercise your option. Other States have the timetable the right way around (namely that we have the review first, then the right to exercise the option), this is not the case in Victorian legislation.

Lease Term: Should the date of commencement of trading be delayed because of the late handover of the premises prior to fit out, then the commencement date and the termination date will be adjusted accordingly.

Storeroom: In the event of a storeroom being supplied as part of the rental, request a licence agreement to be supplied for such storeroom to run concurrently with the lease and to terminate at the same time as the lease.

New Shopping Centres: Gross rental for the new tenancy will be limited to a percentage of sales until such time as the centre is completed. The centre shall be deemed to be completed when all the following have occurred

- All majors are trading
- Car parking is 100% complete
- 95% of the specialty areas are trading or malls to be substantially complete

Cap on Sales to dissolve the lease: We need a provision in the lease that if sales do not reach a specific level of sales by the end of year 2, then the tenant will be entitled to cancel the lease.

CHAPTER 14

Measuring the Value, You Receive for Your Advertising and Catalogue Dollar

One of the major expenses that most retailers usually reduce in a downturn is advertising. However, you cannot stop advertising altogether as the public will soon forget about you. The secret is to spend your advertising dollar to its best advantage.

Firstly, let us look how retailers usually plan their advertising spend so that you can choose the one that suits your needs.

Budgeting for advertising

There are about five major budgeting techniques used by retailers and buying associations today in determining their advertising and promotional budgets:

1. All you can afford procedure

- This is the weakest of the budgeting methods.
- All other retailing costs are accounted for and what is over is placed in your advertising budget.

- Little importance is placed on advertising as a retail mix variable.
- Expenditure is not linked to objectives.
- It is a form of no funds no advertising.
- It is a method used predominantly by small conservative retailers.

2. Arbitrary or historical method

- This method relies on previous budgets. A percentage is added or subtracted from this years budget to determine next year's budget.
- This is a technique useful for small operators.
- It is an easy method to calculate.
- A reference point is thus used as a measurement.
- The budget is adjusted based on your feelings about past success and future trends.
- The disadvantage is that size of budget is rarely tied to specific objectives and evaluation is difficult.

3. The competitive parity method

- The advertising budget is raised or lowered according to the actions of competitors. If a leading retailer in an area raises his advertising by 8%, competitors in the area follow suit.
- It is often used by small and large retailers.
- The advantage is that it provides a point of comparison and is market-orientated.

- The disadvantages are that you are following and not leading.
- It can be difficult to obtain data and so assumptions of similarities in businesses, years in business, size, location, pricing policy and buying group member and so on must be made.

4. Percentage - on - sales technique

- The retailer basis the advertising budget on sales revenue.
- In past years the retailer established an advertising- to- sales ratio of about 3% of sales. In future years, the ratio remains constant and the amount to be spent on advertising varies according to the planned sales for the year.
- The benefits are the use of sales as a base for comparison.
- The shortcomings are that there is no relation to objectives. For an established retailer, an increase in sales may not require an increase in advertising. The advertising dollar spent tends to decrease during poor sales periods, when in fact an advertising boost could be beneficial to sales.
- The technique usually results in too much advertising in periods of high sales and too little advertising in periods of low sales.

5. The objective task method

- With this method the retailer clearly defines his advertising objectives and then determines the size of the budget necessary to satisfy these objectives.

- The number of goals that can be achieved in a year is only limited by the cash resources of the business.
- The advantage is that goals are clearly stated. For example, the cost to establish greater awareness of the store name is decided in advance.
- Expenditure on advertising is related to the completion of goal orientated tasks. Therefore the method is adaptable and success or failure can be evaluated.
- The major shortcoming, is the complexity in setting goals, especially for small retailers.

In determining which of these combinations of techniques you decide to use, you must weigh up the strengths and weaknesses in relation to your individual requirements and constraints. The percentage on sales technique seems to be the most popular method with retailers in Australia.

Planning for advertising

Planning an advertising budget means that you need to think carefully about what results you expect from your advertising. Ask yourself:

- How much money is available for advertising?
- Are you looking for an increase in total sales?
- Are you interested in more sales of a particular product line?
- Are you trying to defend yourself against a competitor?
- If you don't advertise will people still remember that you exist?

TIP: Remember that all the best advertising techniques and objectives in the world are of little value if your store is untidy, your staff is not properly trained to deal with customers and the ambiance of your store does not reflect what you are trying to convey in your advertising message, online website or catalogue. You must get your house in order before you invite visitors to buy your goods.

How to calculate your advertising budget

In order for your advertising dollar to be well spent and achieve its objective in future sales you must look carefully at your products and decide on how much of your advertising dollar to allocate to each. Look at the following example

Example:

Assume your sales budget for next month is $50000 and you basically have 5 product groupings in your store

Product	Sales Target $	% of total sales
1	5000	10
2	20000	40
3	10000	20
4	5000	10
5	10000	20
	50000	100

Assume we are adopting the percentage on sales method and have allocated 5 % of forecasted sales. That is $2500

First look at how much you want to allocate to the budget to achieve your objectives.

Then you allocate the advertising budget to each product line according to its percentage of forecasted sales, that have been adjusted to reflect the specific objectives for the month.

Your objectives for the Month:

1. Products in groups 1 and 5 require normal advertising.
2. Products in group 2 attract co-operative advertising from the manufacturer.
3. You are trying to expand sales of products in group 3.
4. You need to clear excessive stocks of products in group 4.

Allocation of the advertising dollars for the month per product group is thus as follows:

Product line objectives	% of sales	% of advertising	Product line advertising $
1 - normal	10	10	250
2 - plus co-op	40	20	500
3 - expand	20	30	750
4 - overstocked	10	20	500
5 - normal	20	20	500
	100	100	2500

Many retailers also keep a monthly advertising calendar to complete the advertising budget. The calendar should have enough space to record the advertising media planned for each day, the major theme, notes on featured products and most importantly, the cost.

Many retailers also keep information such as sales from the previous year, the number of transactions on a particular day and the theme of last year's advertisements, to help them decide on how to spend their advertising dollar.

Having determined the days of the month that will produce the best results, the best advertising medium for your objectives and the products you want to promote, you will have created a powerful advertising strategy which will maximise the effectiveness of your advertising budget.

Use of catalogues for advertising

Example:

A pharmacy buying group, that services the advertising requirements of a diverse number of pharmacists and geographic locations in Australia, finds that catalogues are their best form of advertising and forms the key to their advertising campaigns.

These catalogues are produced 7 or 8 times a year at specific selling times.

The products to be included in each catalogue are selected by a special committee of members.

Where possible they try to include in their catalogues " shut out" products, that from experience in the past give members the best gross margins.

The catalogues cost about 7 cents each to produce and members can purchase as many as they require to service their area.

As a rule of thumb, sales from catalogues account for about 30 % of sales

Evaluating the performance of a catalogue

In order to asses whether you are receiving value for your advertising dollar, from a catalogue, you must always prepare a profit and loss statement for each catalogue to determine its viability as follows:

Example:

Advertising for a single product retailer.

Sales of product advertised in two weeks prior to catalogue	500
Sales of product advertised in 2 weeks while catalogue in customers homes	1250
Increase in sales directly attributable to catalogue	750
Selling price per product	$100
Gross profit per product normal - 50%	$ 50
Gross profit allowed for in catalogue - 30 %	$30

Profit and loss from Christmas Catalogue

Extra profit generated from catalogue $750 \times \$30 = \$22500$

Less Cost of catalogue

Production $100000 \times 7\text{cents}$	$7000	
Distribution costs	10000	
		= $17000
Extra gross profit generated		$ 5500

In this example, the catalogue was cost effective yielding extra gross profit of $5500.

Remember that as well as the measured value of the catalogue, in the minds of your customers you are reinforcing your name, and your location. And if available, you may have an online website as well.

Always spend according to your cash budget but do not stop spending on advertising.

CHAPTER 15

Managing Your Cash Flow

To survive the squeeze in today's retail climate, cash is king.

Small businesses are especially vulnerable to cash flow problems. Many tend to operate with inadequate reserves, and because they don't put themselves through the discipline of preparing their cash flow statements on a regular basis, they tend to miss the signs of a cash flow deficit until it is too late. Then they find that the stress multiplies. Don't allow yourself to be in this position.

Timing and cash flow are inseparable. Given the seasonal fluctuations experienced in most small retail businesses with the matching of the timing of cash inflows and cash outflows, it's not easy for the small businessperson to function without proper cash flow projections and planning is advisable.

If the cash flow into your business *EXCEEDS* the cash flow out of your business, you can continue to operate and survive. However, if the trend reverses and your business runs out of cash you will soon grind to a halt.

Remember, that even if you have a cash shortfall for a short time and you have not notified your bank well in advance, they may lose faith in your business and in today's tough business environment *"pull the plug"* on you.

The introduction of GST has had a severe impact on cash flows. It was intended to give businesses a cash flow boost as they would collect the GST and use the funds until the GST had to be paid over. However, it is not often used in the way it was intended.

What is the difference between a profit and loss statement and a cash flow statement?

Many small business operators are confused between a" profit and loss statement" and a "cash flow statement". Both use your business's identical numbers but crunch them in different ways for different purposes.

Profit and loss statement

The profit and loss account, which we'll look at shortly, shows how you are using your resources to produce sales.

When examining a profit and loss statement you normally look at 4 items – sales, cost of goods sold, total operating expenses and net profit.

Unless there is a major change in the business operation, these numbers should remain stable from month to month. If the numbers aren't stable, you need to find out why. You may be over-spending, missing discounts, or perhaps you are missing the opportunity to cut costs on a regular basis.

Cash flow statement

Every business plan to make a profit each year. However, you need to know *how cash comes in and goes out of your business.* Cash flow analysis provides the means for you to conduct a periodic check on the financial health of your business.

Preparing a projected cash flow statement, estimates the stream of money that will be coming into the business during the months to come, based on a history of your sales and expenses. The cash flow statement then becomes the core tool for maintaining your control over your business' finances.

Remember, you can show a profit but still be short on cash if a large customer is late in paying.

Like the profit and loss statement, the cash flow statement should be produced monthly. If this isn't possible, you should at least do full quarterly profit and loss and cash flow statements to coincide with the preparation of your BAS return.

To survive, you need to constantly know:

> *Where the money is in your business*
> *Where is the money going?*
> *And how can you get more when you need it?*

Your bank overdraft facilities are there to tide you over the fluctuations within the quarter. A positive cash flow gives you the forward motion to build and grow your business.

A cash flow statement can tell you about the health of your business as well

It is a waste of time preparing a forward cash flow statement if at the end of the month you don't compare your actual cash flow performance with your projected cash flow performance. Even a small lag in sales can have a dramatic impact on your cash flow but you may not know about it if you don't prepare a projected cash flow statement and review it at month end.

Your comparisons between actual and budget may be far out of line because you failed to see, for example, additional casual staff needs over Christmas. Perhaps you missed a major jump in prices from suppliers or even the devaluation of the Australian dollar when your letters of credit on imports were due. **Don't panic!** Cut back on cash outflows, delay payments where possible, ask your suppliers for more time but, more importantly:

Learn the lesson that you must prepare cash flow statements that more realistically meet your needs so that they don't throw up surprises next time.1?

How then do you keep your cash flow under control?

There are four steps to proper cash flow planning:

1. Forecast your income from sales

This forecast is the most important step in cash flow planning. It is your best estimate of your sales split up by month.

It is usually done by taking your last year's sales and adding a percentage. You can then estimate the number of sales you are likely to make multiplied by the average selling price per transaction. This will translate into dollar volume of sales. If you honestly believe that sales will fall because of the retail climate, bite the bullet and make sure that you provide for lower sales in your cash budget.

Since retailers and hospitality businesses mainly sell for cash or on credit cards, your cash inflow from sales will be the same as your sales forecast. If you have some accounts on credit you must then estimate how collections will be made from these accounts.

2. Identify cash outflows

In every business there are expenses that occur on a regular as well as and on an ad hoc basis, and these have to be accounted for. The following items are typical expenses:

Items such as salaries and wages, payments to government departments arising from salary and wage payments like payroll tax, FBT, superannuation as well as normal operating expenses like insurance and light and power costs.

Examine your rent and outgoing outflows. Ask yourself if they are in line with your leases? It is important to determine if this is the case. Also check your lease to see when you are due for a rent review. You will have to take into account the extra rent.

If you are registered for GST on a quarterly basis, you must pay the amounts charged on sales less your input tax credits to the tax office 21 days after each quarter.

As any advertising expenditure such as payment for catalogues or brochures can be anticipated and easily calculated, and must be included in the appropriate month's expenses.

Identify in advance the cost and likely purchase date of capital expenditure items such as replacement of a car or buying a small personal computer. And include in the appropriate month they will be paid for.

Do not forget about your deferred income tax payments for last year or pay as you go payments this year. Your accountant has probably reminded you about them. They must also be included in your cash flow.

This leaves the largest out flow to be identified, namely your purchases. The ratio and analysis we have performed shows that suppliers need to be paid within 30 days to get the maximum discounts. Let's now look at an example.

You are working on a 35% gross profit, your cost of sales will be 65% of your sales payable in arrears. This is explained in the following table.

Example:

Cash flow worksheet to estimate sales, purchases and GST payments for year ended 30 June 2022

Month	Last Year's Sales By Month	% of Total Sales	Sales Budget This Year	10% GST to be added	Gross Profit Of 35%	Purchases 65% of Sales	Month Paid
JULY	108,550	6.5%	121,875	12,188	42,656	79,219	AUG
AUGUST	116,900	7.0%	131,250	13,125	45,938	85,313	SEPT
SEPTEMBER	150,300	9.0%	168,750	16,875	59,063	109,688	OCT
OCTOBER	125,250	7.5%	140,625	14,063	49,219	91,406	NOV
NOVEMBER	167,000	10.0%	187,500	18,750	56,625	121,875	DEC
DECEMBER	233,900	14.0%	262,500	26,250	91,875	170,625	JAN
JANUARY	116,900	7.0%	131,250	13,125	45,938	85,313	FEB
FEBRUARY	100,200	6.0%	112,500	11,250	39,375	73,125	MAR
MARCH	183,700	11.0%	206,250	20,625	72,188	134,063	APRIL
APRIL	141,950	8.5%	159,375	15,938	55,781	103,594	MAY
MAY	91,850	5.5%	103,125	10,313	36,094	67,031	JUNE
JUNE	133,600	8.0%	150,000	15,000	52,500	97,500	JULY
TOTAL	1,670,000	100%	1,875,000	187,500	656,250	1,218,750	

Note: The amount of purchases to be paid in July 2022 is 8% of the previous year'

3. Analyse the net effect of cash flows in and out

(This is easier than it looks...)

Simply summarise the cash flows in and out as per the above example, determining when the major drains are likely to be and how far this is likely to take you over your bank overdraft limits.

Next look at rescheduling your payments so as to" smooth out" the month end "humps".

Keep going... Now you will have to make some important decisions. Should you delay new capital expenditure or approach the tax office to allow you to pay off amounts owing in instalments etc.

4. Arrange facilities with the bank

Alternatively, you may have to ask the bank manager for a temporary facility for a few weeks. When you see your bank manager make sure that you are able to accurately forecast your possible cash defects for the months ahead. He is aware of today's tough times, and if he feels that you are in control of your business, he may be prepared to assist you.

If you have a substantial surplus over the December month end, it would be wise to invest this temporarily to meet the heavy outflow in cash for January and February.

Before you go to see your bank manager for either a temporary overdraft facility or maybe for a loan to refurbish your store as is required under your lease, there are two things you must have

- A cash flow statement for the next 12 months
- A business plan

Now that we have looked at the cash flow statement now we need to look at preparing a business plan

CHAPTER 16

A Typical Business Plan for a Retail Business

In an economic downturn it is essential that any business that wants to remain healthy must have a business plan, that it is revised and revised again as circumstances change. Bankers, suppliers, landlords or others who provide you with credit will most likely ask you produce it before they will advance you any further funding.

To give an accurate picture of how your business operates, your business plan should contain the following points

- An Executive summary
- A summary of the industry in which you operate
- A description of your company and your lease arrangements with your landlord
- An overview of your products and current marketing strategy
- Your customer profile
- Your competition
- Details of the management of the business and its legal and accounting advisers

- Staff profile
- If you are applying for a loan from your bank, you must show how the proceeds of the loan will be spent.
- A financial summary of a 5 year trend of the business to date and how the loan will impact your balance sheet and profit and loss account
- Any other pertinent information the bank or supplier may require

Example

The following is an example of how to prepare a typical business plan for a retail store

SMITH RETAIL SHOE STORE
EXECUTIVE SUMMARY

Smith's Shoes Pty Ltd is seeking a loan of $150,000. The adjacent store is to be taken over to enlarge the existing premises and they wish to use the funding to purchase all fixtures and fittings in respect of those premises to be taken over. They also intend to remove the intervening wall and refurbish the enlarged premises.

Part of the loan will be used to pay off the existing bank loan and to refinance a new loan at the lower interest rates prevailing in Australia at present. The loan will be financed by a first mortgage over the current retail premises owned by the Smith Family.

The Loan will be repaid over five years. It is anticipated that the increased sales resulting from the larger premises will generate sufficient profits to repay it.

The industry in which you operate

Despite the current economic climate in Australia there has been an increase in the demand for footwear sales. The Bureau of statistics has shown a growth of about 3% over the past 12 months. The area of footwear showing the highest growth has been in children's wear and back to school shoes, as well as a demand for high quality walking shoes and athletic footwear.

Due to the limiting size of the store premises, the company has been unable to keep a large enough range of these products to satisfy this demand. An enlargement of the premises would allow them to do this. It is anticipated that current sales could increase by about 30% because of this expansion. With additional products they expect to show a higher gross margin than previously with only conventional men's and ladies shoes.

Company description

Smith's Shoe shop is an independent shoe retail proprietary company. Although it is a single operator, it is well known in Geelong and has been established for some 35 years. The current store managers are the third generation of the Smith family who originally founded the store in 1966.

After leasing the premises for 5 years, the original founder acquired the property at 20 Stumpy Street Geelong, and it has been owned by the family ever since. The property has a mortgage on it of $60000. It was recently valued at $425000. *A copy of such valuation is attached.*

The new premises will be leased from a private landlord for a period of 5 years with two further options of 5 years each at a rental of $18000 per annum.

The existing premises were refurbished some 8 years ago and hence the bank loan outstanding on this refurbishment. The company has repaid the bank to date nearly $80,000 of the original loan plus interest.

PRODUCT OVERVIEW AND CURRENT MARKETING STRATEGY

The stores position in the marketplace

The company operates primarily in the CBD of Geelong and services a passing traffic of about 4 million visitors to the CBD annually. Although known by its family name of Smiths Shoes it is a member of the Australian Buying Group and is thus part of the purchasing power of some 500 stores that operate under that marketing banner throughout Australia. Most of the product is sourced through ABG but some 20% is sourced from their own business connections overseas. This results in higher than normal gross profits.

Although based in Geelong, the company's reputation extends throughout the district. Many of the out-of-town customers visit the store at least once or twice during the year to enjoy the service and range of larger shoe sizes stocked by the company and favoured by many rural customers. These sizes are not usually kept by the national operators and department stores.

The store offers both ladies and men's shoes as well as a small selection of children's and teenage shoes. It stocks a particularly good though limited range of "back to school" shoes in accordance with the requirements of many of the schools in Geelong and district. Again, these shoes are offered in larger sizes beyond that stocked by other competitors.

Customer profile

The demographic profile of Smith's shoppers is unique in that the store enjoys an equal weighting of male and female buyers with a strong bias to younger people. In addition customers are diversified not only by ethnic origin but also increasingly by the changing Australian family profile.

Through on the floor contact and sophisticated computerised analysis, the store is able to monitor the requirements of its customers and changing trends and fashions.

Competition

Smith's Competitors in Geelong can be said to fall under the following classification.

At lower retail price points:	Kmart
	Big W
	Target Country
	Week end Markets
At Middle to Upper price points:	Williams
	Mathers
	Wittners
	Jane Mercer
	Foot Locker

STRATEGY/TACTICS

Management of the Business

The current principals and owners of the business are William and Jeffrey Wright who are the grandchildren of the original owners. William has a business diploma from the University of Ballarat and Jeffrey, after spending a period of 8 years in the shoe manufacturing division of Pacific Dunlop, then joined his brother in the business on the death of his farther.

Both have experience in IT and have set up sophisticated computer systems in the monitoring of the company's stock control, sales analysis and buying functions.

The company has engaged the services of the following advisers.

An Accountant

A retail consultant and lease negotiator

A Solicitor

Staff

At the date of the preparation of this document the company, in addition to its 2 directors, employs a staff of 5 persons, of which 3 are full time and 2 part time over weekends. The 5 staff comprise 4 female shop assistants and 1 male shop assistant.

It is the intention to engage I full time person and 2 part time persons to staff the extra floor space arising out of the enlarged premises. Mr Jeffery Wright is responsible for hiring, training and supervising the staff. The company is undergoing an intense retail training program which has greatly enhanced the staff's selling techniques, add on selling and visual merchandising. It has also installed an online website.

The new staff are also to be involved in the training program. They are all on incentive programs to generate sales and to sell shoes at higher price points than advertised lines.

FINANCIAL DATA:

Application and use of new funds to be raised

The proceeds of the proposed $250,000 loan will be used as follows.

Repayment of Current Loan	$60,000
Fixtures and fittings	$55,000
Additional Working Capital	$135,000
	$250,000

The additional working capital will be invested in stock and staff as well as an advertising campaign on radio to advertise the newly enlarged departments at the store.

Let us now look at an example that will demonstrate how to draw up financial forecasts and projections in a retail store:

THE FINANCIAL FORECASTS AND PROJECTIONS FOR SMITH'S SHOE STORE

Five year sales and profit trend to 30 June 2022

	2018	2019	2020	2021	2022
SALES:	770000	845000	887000	928000	975000
GROSS PROFIT:	40.9	39.9	40.6	40.1	41.1
NET PROFIT PRE TAX:	62005	65030	68809	79804	71787
STOCKTURN:	3.7	3.7	3.8	3.9	4.0

Combined balance sheet at 30 June 2022

	BEFORE FINANCING			AFTER FINANC-ING
	PROP CO	TRADING CO	CON-SOLIDTD	CON-SOLIDTD
ASSETS				
Cash	0	32000	32000	67000
Accounts Receivable	0	33000	33000	33000
Prepaid	0	18000	18000	18000
Stock	0	169000	169000	169000
Total Current Assets	0	252000	252000	287000
Property	450000	0	450000	450000
Motor Vehicles	0	22000	22000	22000
Fixtures and Fittings	0	128000	128000	183000
Office Equip	0	83600	83600	83600
Total Fixed Assets	450000	233600	683600	738600
Total Assets	450000	485600	935600	1025600

	2018	2019	2020	2021	2022
Operating Profit	64487	117400	168350	199200	210900
Disc Recd & Other income	7300	8000	9000	10000	10000
Net Profit Pre Tax	71787	125400	177350	209200	220900
Tax	21536	37620	53205	62760	66270
Net Profit After Tax	50251	87780	124145	146440	154630
% net profit pre tax to sales	7.36	10.45	13.14	14.43	14.73
break even sales	817905	926977	958488	986744	1009535

A final note

Now that you have read this example, have another look at your business plan and try to make it clear and concise without leaving out all the important points about your business functions, management, financials and position in the marketplace.

CHAPTER 17

How to Interact and Communicate with Your Bank Manager

Armed with a cash flow forecast and business plan it is now time to approach your bank manager.

There are many rumours about banks not wishing to make loans to retailers for refurbishments. Naturally this might make you anxious about approaching your bank manager regarding a loan to refurbish your store or for a temporary cash flow facility.

Visiting a bank manager can for some seem as unpleasant as visiting the dentist. But it doesn't have to hurt. When you go to see him you might expect to be grilled on every aspect of the running of your business, and see yourself virtually begging for that extra cash to tide you through. After all, it is his job to protect the bank from a loan that will never be repaid. But it doesn't have to hurt - at least not as much as you think.

Remember that bankers will evaluate you based on your personal and business credibility. The stronger your credit rating the better the terms, interest rates and bank charges you will be able to negotiate.

A bank makes its assessment on granting a business loan on 2 factors- the assets a bank can offer as security, and the reliability and business skills of the management.

From experience in dealing with bankers over a number of years and trying to raise loans, these are some ideas to assist you:

- As well as financial data to back up your request for a loan, provide your bank manager with a simple and clear presentation with graphs and photos where necessary, so that he can fully understand your situation. His staff will then take the time to carefully scrutinise your figures.
- A person who is well prepared with exact figures and working knowledge of current conditions will have a better chance than someone who doesn't. Bankers like confident and exact numbers, not guesses or estimates.
- Think it through and try to anticipate the questions that you will be asked and plan your responses.
- Never give the impression that you are desperate for help. Bankers prefer to loan money to people who don't have to have it. If you don't ask for any concessions and you just sit there, you make a banker nervous. You look too hungry.
- Refuse to allow yourself to be intimidated. Many entrepreneurs carry a false perception that negotiating for a better deal or a lower interest rate may anger the banker and could lead to a denial. Quite the contrary.

- Negotiating strongly with understanding and a frugal attitude to your business will give the banker a positive view of you and your business sense. If he finds you prudent in your approach, he will have less to worry about.

- Begin your negotiations with a discussion about interest first, and then talk terms. This is important since your efforts to negotiate good terms can be easily offset by a banker holding the line on interest. Of course, if terms are more important to you, then start with this. Always nail down what is most important first and then concede the lesser points.

- Many bankers will not directly offer to help you to qualify for the loan. Though they have the information and they are often willing to advise you and assist in several ways, they will not volunteer their assistance. You have to ask.

- If you find yourself frustrated with hypothetical scenarios, try something like this *"Okay you've told me all the ways this will not work. You're the expert. How can we make it work"* or *"If you were in my shoes, what would you do?"*

- If you know you are close but a junior bank official has denied your loan, you may do some intimidating of your own by going over his or her head. Just threatening to appeal may be sufficient. Nobody likes customers to take problems to their boss.

- Don't be afraid to tell your banker your most intimate (business) secrets. He will probably have forgotten by the time you leave his office, but he will remember that you took him into your confidence about what is really happening in your business.

Applying for a loan and getting a good interest rate

The Federal Reserve Bank in Australia sets the basis for the calculation of interest rates on all borrowings. It initiates the process by announcing the new bank rate that it proposes to charge the commercial banks. The commercial banks then announce the new overdraft rate it will charge its customers.

Remember that when you ask the bank for a loan you will not be charged the same rate that the bank offers major customers who frequently borrow money. When you see advertisements by banks quoting rates for services, this is the rate for customers like BHP, WOOLWORTHS, and SHELL OIL, not the rate for the average small business owner.

A small business is charged about 3 to 6 percentage points above this rate depending on its credit worthiness and, *in the opinion of the bank,* the ability of the small business to repay borrowings.

What factors does a bank manager take into account when approving a loan?

Let's look at the situation from the other side of the desk. This will help you in your request for a loan and your negotiations with the bank manager.

Any bank manager will begin from a defensive position, wanting to protect the lenders from shonky deals that could suck the bank's lifeblood. He carries an onerous responsibility and for this reason it is up to you to give a good impression. You should be seen as organised, hardworking and your paperwork must be correct. The degree you will be hassled and grilled depends largely on how you present yourself as a disciplined and committed operator of a viable small business.

Bankers and all people who lend money to businesses consider at least the following factors:

- Convincing evidence that the loan will be repaid.
- Convincing evidence that indicates that you can manage your affairs well enough to ensure the paying back of the loan.
- Convincing evidence that you are sufficiently committed to the business for the bank to feel sure that you will work hard to protect it and make it grow.
- In the worst scenario, if your business fails, the banker needs to feel certain that the value of the business is such that on a disposal of the business, the bank will get their money back.

What proportion of the cash or equity should be contributed by the borrower to the capital cost of any project?

How do you deal with your banker to acquire your loan?

Whether you are having your annual review of your banking facilities, wish to apply for a loan to refit your premises as required under your lease, or perhaps invest in more stock, the following points should be kept in mind when dealing with your banker, so as to achieve the desired result at the lowest possible cost:

- Bankers are impressed only by your standards of management excellence.
- Experience counts heavily in planning, organising, supervising, directing, developing and demonstrating success in your business.
- Arrange your borrowing needs well in advance and keep time on your side. You may be able to shop around. Banks are in competition with each other and you may find an alternate bank willing to negotiate terms such as security margins, interest rates and collateral requirements.

Risk taking must be a calculated decision and the endeavour should not be a speculative gamble. Remember that bankers are risk avoiders and not risk takers!

Give the bank manager all the information he requires for head office approval of a loan. Although the preparation for a visit to the bank may seem like an enormous amount of work, you'll find that going well prepared pays excellent dividends.

You should provide him with the following evidence that you will be able to repay the loan through the normal running of your business:

That the loan is big enough to do the job and you won't have to come back for more;

- A business plan.

- Cash flow projections for the first 12 months including repayment plans.
- A profit and loss for the first and second year
- List of assets if any are offered as collateral for the loan.
- A short history of your business experience
- Your debt paying record in the past.

You need to also take the following into consideration:

Try to negotiate your financial credit needs at your year-end while your financial statements are still correct. Annually arrange a line of credit to meet peak requirements and borrow only what is necessary, when necessary.

- Adjust the loan level as your actual requirements change.
- Make realistic repayment commitments.
- Borrow loans from banks only for specific projects since interest rates on such loans are often cheaper than bank overdrafts.

The bank will usually accept the following as collateral.

- A floating charge or debenture over the entire business.
- Personal guarantees of the proprietor or all partners.
- Outside guarantors like the retailer's main supplier acting as a guarantor.
- The pledging of cash surrender value of life policies.
- The agreement to restrict salaries, drawings and loan repayment of proprietors, partners or shareholders.

- A mortgage on property if available.
- Collateral over intangible assets that do not appear on the balance sheet.

As one of your conditions for the loan, suggest that your bank manager visit your business. Pick him up if necessary. It's a good idea to take your manager out for a friendly lunch at least every 12 months, to keep the bank informed of how you are doing and what's new in your industry or profession. Good relationships between banker and client are essential and worth the expense and effort.

Remember this is your last option when you have nothing else to lose. If this does not work, then it's time to move to a new bank

In summary:

- Bankers are almost by nature cautious and conservative particularly in the current financial climate in 2023..
- Any misleading information, once determined, will destroy the all-important mutual trust required.
- Experience clearly shows that business owners, who keep their bankers informed of their successes and lack of it, get the best co-operation when having difficulties.
- Your banker should expect your business to have financial peaks and valleys. So should you!
- Banking is basically "you give me what I need and I will give you what you need". But be sure of what you need and what you are prepared to pay for it.

- Try to plan your financing so that your proposal does not appear "desperate".
- Planning is a management quality. It is also a significant criterion for loan proposals. "Urgent" proposals show a weakness in management.
- Never surprise your banker with sudden or unplanned requests for funds.
- Applying for commercial credit can be tedious. It calls for more documentation than you might have initially expected. Don't be disheartened by the amount of paper work needed to accompany the application. Instead, be prepared.

CHAPTER 18

Stock Shrinkage and How to Stop It Happening in Your Store

With the times as they are at present and as people run out of money, it is inevitable that some will resort to shoplifting. This in turn could result in major stock shrinkage in your store.

Remember you are in business for two reasons. Firstly, to give a service to the public and secondly, to sell goods at a profit.

You are not in business for theft by your own staff or the shopping public. Neither are you prepared to be the victim of fraudulent or dishonest practices.

The open market concept of retailing, where goods are attractively displayed and customers are invited to personally select what catches their eye, leaves most retailers open prey to professional or amateur shoplifters. A recent report by Checkpoint Security, annual Global Theft Barometer, shows that Australia loses at least $2 billion a year in stock shrinkage. This makes up 1.4% of total retail sales in 2010 and is likely to rise further during the present economic decline.

Where does stock shrinkage occur in your business?

According to Checkpoint Security, shrinkage occurs most frequently in the following areas of your business

Through your employees	40.6%
As a result of shoplifting	36.8%
From internal errors	17.3%
Through suppliers and vendors	5.3%
	100.0%

Even putting shop lifting aside, internal theft remains Australian retailers' biggest loss?

Other studies point out four major differences between retailers with low and high pilferage rates:

1. Retailers with low pilferage are tougher when they apprehend persons caught stealing.
2. They are more likely to prosecute all shoplifters.
3. Low - shrinkage retailers are more conscientious in keeping records of supplier shortages in deliveries;
4. Retailers who minimise shortages set up systems to prevent employee theft.

Australian Retailers are starting to install more sophisticated overnight CCTV systems in stores. Loss prevention methods also include EAS, RFID and analytics, and the use of video verification products. Internet protocol cameras are being used more frequently making it easier for police to identify and now prosecute offenders.

ADT Security has identified "sweet hearting" as a major factor in lost retail revenue. According to its research 43% of small businesses admit that they or their colleagues provide discounts or freebies to friends and family. The survey showed that the younger the employee the more likely they were to engage in this practice.

Measuring the true extent of our loss due to shrinkage

Things aren't always the way they seem – analyse your stock shrinkage carefully.

Having taken stock and ascertained that the gross profit achieved is not what you expected, you could very easily conclude that you have been the victim of stock shrinkage. The best approach is to stop thinking of shortages in terms of gross sales.

If you talk of a shortage of 1.5% of sales, it does not sound too bad or serious but in reality shrinkage has nothing to do with gross sales, it is in fact a *"direct and actual reduction from net profit"*

A one-dollar article stolen is a one-dollar loss from the bottom line net profit

Take a closer look

To determine the "real" loss you must calculate how many articles you will have sell to:

1. Recover the cost of the article stolen
2. 2. Recover the profit that would have been made if the article had not been stolen but sold.

The following example shows how the real loss is calculated.

Example 1

In a store, a baby's dummy is stolen

Dummy cost	$1 - 50
Sold for	$2 - 00
Profit	$0 - 50

Question:

How many baby's dummies must the retailer sell to recover the cost of the stolen dummy and the profit that would have been made on it if it had not been stolen?

Answer:

The retailer must sell 4 baby dummies

However, the time and wages involved in selling the extra 4 dummies can never be recovered - "they are a dead loss".

Reasons for shrinkage

Experience in the retail industry has shown there to be many reasons for stock losses. The following is a checklist of major errors resulting in inventory shortage:

A. Errors by sales assistants

- The wrong retail price on customer's invoice or cash
- register docket. Or ringing up the wrong price on the cash register.
- Failure to record regular markdowns on correct forms.
- Failure to take markdowns on exchanged merchandise returned from customers as defective, as a loss.
- Failure to take markdowns on window damaged goods as a loss.
- Errors in additions on sales dockets.
- Lost "chargeable account" sales dockets.
- Guessing at the price of merchandise that has no price ticket.
- On measured items, sales assistant gives the customer extra merchandise "for good measure".
- Returned merchandise that is not correctly re-marked at the sold price and then returned to stock at the current price, which may be lower.
- Improper recording of lay-bys.
- Returns to suppliers without getting the appropriate credit note.

- Sales recorded on wrong PLU.
- Sales of multiples (eg 2 for $3.50) processed as 1 for $3.50.
- Computer cost files corrupted by " averaging" and by human intervention.
- Regrouping of a number of items under a common PLU.
- Incorrect input of cost and selling prices on the point of sale register.
- Incorrect use of "no sale" controls on the register.

B. Errors in handling merchandise

- Pricing merchandise differently to the amount shown on the invoice. This happens when advertised merchandise at reduced prices is received during a sale.
- Incoming merchandise is not counted accurately or there is a failure to keep records of goods returned.
- With staff collusion and access to scrap bins, merchandise can easily be placed in boxes and then removed from the store.
- Using stock for internal purposes without charging it to an expense account.
- Approving both the original and duplicate invoice for payment.
- If a retailer owns more than one store, goods can be lost in transit between stores.
- Failure to send claim forms to the accounting office for short deliveries,

- Supplier's representatives may pick up merchandise for replacement but fail to replace them.
- Old price tags incorrectly placed onto new stock items.
- Theft from the "back door" after stock has been delivered and recorded but before it is transferred to the stock room or display area.

Alert staff can help to stop shoplifters

Sales staff the key to prevent shoplifting.

- Staff should be trained to be assertive, confident, and aware.
- They should serve all customers as quickly as possible.
- Even when the store is busy, customers should be acknowledged as soon as they come into the store. This alerts potential shoplifters that you know they are there.
- Sales staff should check back regularly with customers who wish to browse. Legitimate customers will appreciate the opportunity to ask questions, while shoplifters will feel watched and may leave.
- The salesperson should never turn their back on a customer or leave the sales area unattended. They should develop a warning or alert system to communicate the presence of a suspected shoplifter.
- Employees should be trained to handle cash so they can't be talked into giving change for a larger bill than was actually offered or giving change twice, or exchange money with a con artist.

- Arrange an alert system with other traders in your area so that everyone knows when a suspected shoplifter is working your area.

During difficult times like at present reducing stock shrinkage is vital

CHAPTER 19

Efficient Product Buying and How to Maximise Your Profit from Each Square Metre of Space in Your Store

As buyer in your retail business, you must buy in the most efficient manner, ensuring that you maximize the store's profit from each square metre available in your store.

Let us now look at how you can improve the efficiency rating of each line and each department.

INDIVIDUAL LINES

To ensure the best profit per line within your store the most important factors to consider are *the initial mark-ups on merchandise and gross profit after markdowns.*

As the buyer of product for your business, you are constantly being called upon to assess the efficiency rating of:

- Selected promotional lines
- High volume sell lines
- High stock lines

A tough market

Today's market is highly competitive. You must market your product against similar products sold by the supermarkets, discount department stores or big specialist stores. Often the only way to compete is with home brand or exclusive products.

It is often hard to decide which line will sell best. Rather than using gut instinct, to make that decision, apply the reliable and tested strategy of efficiency ratios.

AN EFFICIENCY RATIO

The formula for this ratio is as follows:-

STOCK TURN RATE X 2 PLUS REQUIRED GROSS PROFIT

Example:

In this example we are looking at the efficiency of 3 different lines

	Line A	Line B	Line C
Stock turn rate	3	4	6
Multiplied by 2	6	8	12
Planned gross profit, say	40	38	34
Efficiency rate	46	46	46

Stock turns are multiplied by 2 since most fashion retailers will have at least two seasons per year. If you are not a fashion retailer, then ignore step 2 and do not multiply by 2.

A line with a high stock turn rate but a lower gross profit can be equal to an item with a low stock turn rate but high gross profit. So, in deciding which line to buy, always select the one with the highest efficiency rating or the one that gives you the most money in the bank. The line with the highest gross profit is often not the one that provides the most money in the bank.

This technique can be used for the rating of each department in your store as well and it should be carried out at least every quarter.

To keep ahead of your competition, a department which consistently rates low on the efficiency rating system should be closed.

How to maximise your profit from each square metre of space in your store

Example

Although retail sales or profits may rise or fall, there is one constant in your business and that is *the size of you store*. The cost of renting this area is expensive. To simplify calculations, we will express the total occupancy costs of the retailer at, say, $400 per square metre when comparing it with other retailers.

When comparing similar businesses of differing sizes, we can then express sales at say $8,500 per square metre. In this way we can bring the comparison to a common form of measurement. It is then easily understood by others.

A very useful management technique is to measure the performance of the business as it relates to the sales and the gross profit earned by each department each month according to the area that we have allocated to that department.

The following example is of a typical pharmacy by department. It clearly shows the performance of each department.

TYPICAL PHARMACY: ANALYSIS OF SALES BY TRADING AREA YEAR ENDING JUNE 2022

Front of Shop Analysis

DEPARTMENT	SIZE Sq. Mtr	SALES FOR YEAR	GROSS PROFIT YEAR	SALES AS % OF FRONT OF SHOP	GROSS PROFIT AS % FRONT OF SHOP	SIZE AS % FRONT OF SHOP	SALES RATING BY VALUE	GP RATING BY VALUE	RATING DEPT BY SIZE
Coughs & Colds	5.25	104,732	42,945	14.68	16.57	4.35	1	1	9
Skin Care	6.60	97,554	33,168	13.68	12.80	5.47	2	2	7
Syringes	1.00	64,000	27,600	8.97	10.65	0.83	3	3	24
General Medicine	1.60	62,647	23,926	8.78	9.23	1.33	4	4	20
Analgesics	3.00	53,167	18,545	7.45	7.16	2.49	5	5	13
Hair Care	6.00	36,036	12,621	5.05	4.87	4/98	6	7	8
Baby	12.00	35,774	14,310	5.02	5.52	9.95	7	6	1
Vitamins	4.50	35,646	10,393	4.86	4.01	3.73	8	8	10
Eye & Ear	1.30	24,482	8,079	3.43	3.12	1.08	9	9	23
Fragrance	9.00	21,134	7,396	2.96	2.85	7.46	10	10	4
Stomach & Gut	3.00	20,943	6,701	2.94	2.59	2.49	11	11	14
Wound Care	4.50	16,282	4,884	2.28	1.88	3.73	12	15	12
Mens	7.50	15,696	5,965	2.20	2.30	6.22	13	12	6
Sports Medicine	4.50	13,988	5,315	1.96	2.05	3.73	14	14	11
Other	10.50	12,686	5,708	1.78	2.20	8.71	15	13	3
Womens Cosmetics	9.00	12,007	3,602	1.68	1.39	7.46	16	18	5

DEPARTMENT	SIZE Sq. Mtr	SALES FOR YEAR	GROSS PROFIT YEAR	SALES AS % OF FRONT OF SHOP	GROSS PROFIT AS % FRONT OF SHOP	SIZE AS % FRONT OF SHOP	SALES RAT-ING BY VALUE	GP RAT-ING BY VAL-UE	RAT-ING DEPT BY SIZE
Photographics	0.75	9,863	2,465	1.38	0.95	0.62	17	20	27
Misc/Cash Desks	11.75	9,120	3,648	1.28	1.41	9.74	18	17	2
Oral Hygiene	1.80	8,384	1,677	1.18	0.65	1.49	19	24	18
Confectionary	1.00	7,968	3,984	1.12	1.54	0.83	20	16	25
Family Planning	0.50	7,685	1,537	1.08	0.59	0.41	21	26	30
Foot Care	0.75	7,115	2,277	1.00	0.88	0.62	22	21	28
Asthma	2.25	6,527	2,611	0.92	1.01	1.87	23	19	17
Sun Care	1.50	6,079	2,128	0.85	0.82	1.24	24	22	21
Antacids	3.00	5,605	1,905	0.79	0.74	2.49	25	23	15
Household	0.75	5,512	1,543	0.77	0.60	0.62	26	25	29
Hand & Nails	1.50	5,430	1,358	0.76	0.52	1.24	27	27	22
Home Health Care	3.00	3,520	1,056	0.49	0.41	2.49	28	29	16
Diabetes	1.80	3,030	1,212	0.42	0.47	1.49	29	28	19
Feminine Hygiene	1.00	1,692	609	0.24	0.23	0.83	30	30	26
TOTAL FRONT OF SHOP	120.60	713,305	259,168	100.00	100.	100.00			
DISPENS – GOVT	25.40	1,570,000	669,824						
DISPENS – PATIENT		523,695							
TOTAL PHARMACY	146.00	2,807,000	928,992						

Analysis of pharmacy layout sales and profitability

- The department with the largest area, namely baby products, produces the 7th highest sales and the 6th highest gross profit.
- The cash desks which are meant for impulse and miscellaneous products such as lollies and so on, and usually carry high mark-ups, are obviously not working for the pharmacy as they rank only 17th in gross profit.
- Two of the smallest departments, namely syringes and general medicine, are the 3rd and 4th best in both sales and gross profit.
- Two high profile departments, namely diabetes and feminine hygiene, perform worst in the pharmacy.

Clearly the pharmacy has not been laid out in a way that maximises sales and profitability.

More space needs to be allocated to successful departments in the front of the shop and less space allocated to less profitable departments. Unfortunately though not profitable some departments may have to be maintained due to customer needs and demands.

CHAPTER 20

Is Your Supplier Giving You a Good Deal?

You may buy product from a supplier who generally services you and other similar retailers in your category, but is he a good supplier and do his products help you achieve the overall gross margin you are trying to achieve in your business?

Often you find when dealing with a supplier, for you to achieve at least a further 10% reduction in cost you may have to buy 6 of a product. You do so and at the end of the season you are left with say 2 of those items. Finally, you have to get rid of those products at well below cost. Thus you are driving down your gross margin.

How to measure the performance of your supplier

One of the best techniques for monitoring the performance of a supplier is to include a two-digit supplier code into each stock item's code number. Thus, from your stock control system, when producing a quarterly or 6 monthly, or even a seasonal trading account, you will be able to take out a trading account by major supplier.

Example:

If the strategy of your business is to mark up the cost of each product by 100%, you will be making a first gross profit of 50%.

You also know from past experience with sales, markdowns and shrinkage, that this gross profit is reduced to 42%. It is also the basis you used to set your budget for the year or season.

It follows that if you take out a trading account for a supplier whose product you can track through the stock system by his code number; it will show the following result for the season

Supplier A

Sales of Shoes for season	$50000
Less Cost of sales	32000
Gross profit	18000
% Gross profit to sales	36%
Budget % Gross profit to sales	42%

As you can see from this example, this supplier is not suitable for your business.

Suggestion:

The next time you meet with this supplier discuss the following:

- Show him his seasonal account of his supply to you.

- Point out to him how using your open programme, you were forced to discount the last unsold items of his product at the end of the season to clear stock, and that this has had a major impact on your gross margin.

- Suggest to him that you can only continue using him as a supplier if he gives you an extra 10% on 3 products (not 6). In this way you will be avoiding the loss of extra margin at the end of the season.

- Or even suggest that it is time to negotiate a new price structure if he wishes to remain a supplier with your retail business.

Know your suppliers and you will be surprised at what better buying deals you can achieve.

CHAPTER 21

Growing Your Business Successfully

The balance sheet of a company is often compared to a sponge. The sponge absorbs water while the balance sheet soaks up cash. As the sponge nears its capacity to absorb additional water it becomes increasingly less efficient. The same occurs with your business.

Increasing sales or growth creates a need for additional money to finance an increased level of assets. Although the business may attract an injection of funds by the owner, injecting capital or taking in a partner, the main source of finance is from debt. This is a risky business. Any increase in interest expenses could put pressure on profits.

Growth in sales is often accompanied by a decrease in efficiency of operation. Proportionately, more assets are required to support new sales so that the rate of assets growth increases faster than sales - you make the same percent of profit but you make it less efficiently.

Smarter and better

If you want to survive this economic downturn and expand your business successfully, you must manage growth better. One method of achieving this is by adopting the following management techniques:

- Manage your current assets, particularly stock and stock-turns, more efficiently.
- Restructure your debt between long term and short-term debt.
- Sell your unproductive assets.
- Close your inefficient departments within the business.
- Control your expansion program. Each growth step is evaluated before proceeding with the next one.
- Lease instead of buying your assets.
- Implement sale and leaseback of your existing assets.
- Accept the concept of more risk.
- Bring in a partner.

Be proactive

It is a human failing that we wait until we are sick before we go to the doctor or in Australian terms "If it ain't broke don't fix it". We normally wait for the symptoms to appear and then respond to problems. Sometimes this is too late.

We love to call this the Australian entrepreneurial spirit, the 'gut feel' approach or 'going for broke.' There is nothing wrong with this attitude, but we need to put it into a structure and framework that capitalises on our business strengths and shores up the business weaknesses.

Skin deep

Problems in your business are solved when you examine the deeper causes. As in medicine, treating the symptoms of a disease alone won't cure it.

> *Business owners often erroneously blame the poor health of their business on low cash, low gross margin, and low net profit. What an excuse for poor business management and performance!*

If you study the information provided and apply it, hopefully in time you will turn your present difficulties around and emerge as a more organised and financially viable small business. More importantly, your resilience will enable you to survive the peaks and troughs of an ever-changing financial climate for small business in Australia.

PART 2

EXITING FROM YOUR BUSINESS

CHAPTER 22

The Decision to Retire and Exit from Your Business

Are you reaching the stage of life when you wish you could escape the everyday confines of your business, play golf or be out on the bay? Or are you a franchisee who has had enough of franchising and would like to move on?

Don't walk away from something you've spent so much of your time and energy establishing. Approach this change in your business life like all others, in a logical and planned manner. In this way you can achieve the most from it.

The following chapters will take you through the many aspects that you and your family need to carefully consider and review before it is time for you to call in your lawyer or financial planner.

What are the main options facing the owner when he decides to leave the business?

When an owner of a business leaves, he or she has 3 options and each of these brings its own problems.

1. Sell the Business

2. A management buyout by staff
3. Keeping it in the family.

Sale of business

- If you sell the business, you will realise its value without the demand of transition.
- However, the owner must be ready to disengage from the business almost immediately.
- Sometimes new owners will ask the current owner to stay on in an advisory capacity and the owner will have to learn to deal with the style of the new management.
- A sale would require the business to be put ready for sale and due diligence by a new owner. We will deal in more detail with this later on.

Management buyout

- This will give your existing staff even more incentive to further the business' profitability.
- It may be a good strategy for the existing owner to remain on as a board member or having a less active role, without walking away from the business completely.
- There would be less argument as to price as all parties are privy to the company's progress, strengths and weaknesses. They would also have relatively similar views on its value.
- Banks may be happy to support this, as it involves less risk than with new or unfamiliar management.

Keeping it in the family

- This can be a difficult proposition particularly for large families and the aspirations of the potential heirs.

- Communication is the essential ingredient and the need to cater for those family members who will miss out, must be handled with the utmost delicacy.

- The equal share basis may not always be the best way to go. A business must have people who can assume leadership, make quick decisions and ensure that the business is focused on its objectives. Management by committee does not always allow for this.

- The different talents and capabilities of all heirs should be fully and unemotionally resolved. The need to broaden the experience of successors, who may have technical but not financial backgrounds, should also be fully explored.

- The possibility of a successor working in another company in the industry to broaden his skills should also be considered.

- The use of a form of mentoring offered by many companies to assist the overall skills of the individuals, who will be running the company in the future, should be considered.

So why do many retailers have trouble facing the issue of sucession planning?

With the ageing of the Australian population, many owners of retail businesses may be faced with having to plan for retirement and ensuring an orderly succession to the next generation.

History tells us that family-owned businesses fail more often then they succeed. The average life cycle of a family business is 27 years, which means that all too many family orientated businesses never make it past the first generation.

Many Australian small businesses tend to put succession planning on the back burner. This is probably the reason why 70% of small family businesses never make it to the second generation. Only 13% are run by grandchildren and less than 3% are run by great grandchildren.

These statistics show that that much of family wealth created in the first generation is frequently lost by the third generation. There are many reasons put forward for this phenomenon:

- There is often a perceived conflict in values and beliefs between generations about leadership styles.
- Succeeding generations that now own the business, may experience family problems such as divorce or the death of a spouse. A family problem soon becomes a business problem, particularly if these new owners can't fulfill their obligations in their management roles.

The only way for a sustainable cross generation family business to succeed is to have continuity. This must be consciously led and managed and can best be achieved by:

- Maximizing effective communication through shared values and building a sense of community.

- Growing the family's human and intellectual capital.
- Mentoring the existing family members to build confidence in their new roles and eliminate any management weaknesses.

Retirement is hard to envisage when there is still so much to do and succession planning has a ring of finality to it.

A study conducted by KPMG in 2009, showed that for most family businesses, succession planning is a key issue. It raises sensitive issues about the future of the business, the potential crystallisation of tax liabilities, the distribution of wealth accumulated in the business and the relationships between family members.

Only 15% of the surveyed businesses reported having a formal business plan, although 31% said that they were currently working on one. In addition over 40% of respondents intended to pass on the business to the next generation or other family members. Nearly 20% admitted to having changed their succession plans during the previous 12 months.

It is possible that the recent financial crisis may well have delayed succession moves in some businesses by increasing uncertainty and reducing financial flexibility.

Statistics show that despite the world economic crisis, over the next 5 years more than 50% of Australian family business CEO's will retire. Only about 65% have identified their successor and just 25% have a documented succession plan in place.

Even though you may be thinking through a succession plan, and you feel that the future of your business is safe, you will soon find out that adequate succession planning is far more complex than you imagine.

There are 4 major areas of risk that may upset the most well intended planning:

- Death or illness can come to managers when they least expect it.
- You may not be able to leave the business when you want to for financial or other reasons.
- You may not be able to realise the maximum value of the business when you decide to leave.
- You may not be able to keep the business running without actively being present.

How you manage these risks depends on your personal objectives. There is no one size fits all succession plan

What does having a succession plan signal to the outside world?

By carefully planning the next step for your business, you will be sending a signal to the trade, to your competitors and to the bankers who supply finance to your business, that your business is expected to be successful and thrive into the next generation.

This signal indicates that the next generation has been trained and can take over the business in the event of the retirement or demise of the current owner. Bankers in particular feel comfortable when such a plan is in place particularly in the current retail climate.

A plan will help to clarify the hopes and aspirations of the successors. It will highlight estate planning and retirement issues at an earlier stage when action can still be taken.

Creating an ongoing legacy

Good succession planning takes care of you, your family and the community that may rely on your business. It is about laying the foundations for the longevity of the business after you have gone and it secures an exit deal that is good for you and the people you care about. Good succession planning caters for all that occurs in the business that is both the expected and the unexpected.

A plan is best made early, reviewed regularly and should be based on sound independent and expert advice.

CHAPTER 23

Are You Ready for Succession?

Don't just jump into succession planning. Take your time. Answer the following checklist before deciding if this is the path you would like to take and whether you are ready for it.

- Do you view your business as a family business?
- Do you want your business to remain a family business? If so, why and how will you go about it?
- Do you have potential successors in mind who are willing and able to manage the business? Are these plans clearly defined?
- Does the business have plans for the career development of successor members? If so, what are they?
- If you want fair play, does the business have a formal appraisal and remuneration system for family and non-family members?
- Do you have written personal, family, business and succession plan in place?
- Do your plans cover unforseen events?
- Do your plans include death, disability and business continuity insurance policies? If so, what are these details?

- Is the business adequately resourced and staffed to cope with growth in the long term as well as the short term?
- Do you have a board of directors or advisory board to guide the younger business owner and help him/her where required?
- Do you have agreed processes for handling conflicts between family and business issues and between family members? If so, what are they?

If most of your answers are positive and you have a clear and logical plan for future succession, you are ready to take the next step and look at implementation.

Establish a suitable structure for your business

Whether your eventual goal is selling the business or finding a new manager, either from your family, or from external sources (but retaining ownership and some level of income), you will need to structure the company so that it can function without you.

This structure will entail the following:

- Formal governance systems.
- Well documented systems and processes.
- Formal contracts to lock in key staff, customers, and suppliers.
- Registering all your intellectual property and trade names.
- Having a secure long-term lease in place.

Depending on the size of your business, there are some other considerations before embarking on your plans. These include the following:

- Do you have a clear retirement plan? Has this plan been implemented?
- Is your retirement income adequately funded?
- Does your family and business have a clear mission statement or policy charters? If so, what are they?
- Have you discussed your succession plans with your spouse?
- Does your spouse share your vision of the future?
- What are the largest risks to your business?
- How are you managing the aspirations of your staff?
- Do you have in place a business plan and cash forecast for the company to cover the short and long term projections of the business?
- Do you know how to structure your business to get the best tax outcome from the sale?
- What sort of management information do you generate every month?

If your answer is NO to many of these questions, you may have some thinking to do followed by planning. If your plan is to sell the business, you will need to put in the time to prepare the business to stand up to a significant due diligence test from a buyer. Purchasers are all too aware that in a small business most of the goodwill sits with the owner.

Setting the date for your retirement with your family

- The first step in succession planning is setting a retirement date target.

- The next step involves a meeting of the family to discuss your retirement and its implications.

- Simply walking away is not a solution. This is a family decision and joint project in which everyone starts to mentally prepare for the retirement of the owner.

- Every family business is different, and you have to now separate business issues from personal issues. For example, sale to a brother could upset the owner's son or the brother's children.

- Once the retirement date has been set, some estate planning considerations can be put into place in consultation with legal and financial advisers.

- Having enough money to retire on, may drive succession planning. This may be the case if the principal feels that more money can be raised by either selling the business or listing it on the stock exchange (if large enough) rather than by bequeathing to children with a guaranteed income stream from the business.

- A good succession plan could take a number of years to prepare and implement and once agreed upon, all the family must be committed to it.

CHAPTER 24

Mentoring Family Members

We all know of successful businesses where children have followed in a father's footsteps and within a short period of time the business has failed or has been sold short of its value. *This is not what you want for your business.*

One of the questions facing a company that decides on a likely successor for the current CEO from the family unit, is will the new person have the capabilities and management skills to run the business as well as the existing CEO.

The new person may have strong selling or buying skills but lacks financial skills. The sudden mantle of leadership may be overwhelming. No one can know or do it all. Mentors and mentoring that has been around since the beginning of time can help you to educate the successor in areas of deficiency.

What is mentoring and how can you find the correct mentor?

A mentor is simply a role model to consult for advice, guidance, and support.

There are many mentors offering their services in Australia. But before engaging one, you need to assess and consider the strengths and weaknesses of the potential new CEO, both generally and from a business perspective. Only then can you conclude the way in which a mentor may help the new CEO to grow both personally and professionally.

- It may also be worth considering what sort of person you are and the type who compliments you.
- Possibly the hardest part of the mentoring process will be finding a genuine and talented mentor. A number of government authorities provide successful business people to mentor small business people.
- Informal mentoring relationships can also be extremely beneficial. A good idea is to network and join industry associations and make contacts. You will identify businesses you admire and then consider contacting them.
- When you discover someone with whom you would like to develop a mentoring relationship, take things slowly. First ask that person to lunch or send them an email that asks a specific question. Gauge the attractiveness of the person as a mentor based on their response and the value of their advice. Just as you do not propose marriage to somebody on the first date, you should not ask somebody if they will be your mentor straight away.
- Remember working with a mentor is the best way to get an unofficial business education. Therefore, it is essential that you can feel that you can be open and honest with this

person. You need to feel free to ask them your questions. They need to understand your dreams for the business.

- Ultimately, the level of communication you have with your mentor will determine the success of the relationship.

- The mentoring relationship usually lasts from about 6 months to a year. If you are grooming a successor to a family business this could last for 5 years. There is nothing to stop you cultivating another relationship with another mentor who meets your changing needs and the needs of your business.

- While you soak up your mentor's knowledge, you cannot simply meet with them, sit in a chair and hope that their knowledge will transfer to you like a sponge. Make the most of your limited time with your mentor by dealing with two or maybe three issues at the most that you want help with. Work on the knowledge you have gained and assess your progress together.

CHAPTER 25

Succession and Retirement Techniques That Make Full Use of Your Retail Lease

Before leaving a business always consider the range of techniques available to you that could boost the financial viability of your business. The following are some suggestions that you might think about and then discuss with your accountant or lawyer.

Using your retail lease to maximum advantage

As the lease is often the single item that under-pins the value of your business, you need to examine it and ask yourself the following questions:

- Do I have a solid retail lease, and does it maximize its value in the business?
- What will the buyer of a business be looking for when conducting the proper due diligence on an existing lease?
- If the retail store is located on real estate owned by me, how can I improve the value of that real estate by using my lease?

- Can I use the conditions of the lease to create a better tax effective dissolution of a partnership?

Getting the lease in order with a view to a sale of your business

As indicated earlier, just as you need to have a good lease entering a business, so you need to ensure that you have a good lease exiting the business. The buyer's solicitor will be looking at several key items in the lease in order to determine this.

The following are key issues which makes the lease a good lease for a new buyer:

- It should have at least 5 years to run until the end of the current lease term.
- If possible, it should have an option for one or two additional lease terms. Such options should be totally unrestricted in their ability to be exercised.
- If your lease has only a short time to go, no buyer trying to assess the potential of the business will be prepared to pay for goodwill knowing that within a short period he may no longer have a lease.
- If you have an old lease which commenced before the introduction of changes to state acts, ensure that the outgoings clause does not have a provision requiring you to pay for the shortfall in outgoings not paid by the major tenants.
- Ensure that any market review clauses have no "ratchet clauses" which only allow rental to rise following a review.

In tough times market rentals usually fall. The new rental determined by a market review must be allowed to fall to this new level.

- Ensure that clauses dealing with repainting and restoration are not at fixed intervals but "as and when necessary."

- Ensure that no immediate fit out of the business is required on assignment, as this will be considered by a potential buyer in assessing the purchase price for the retail business.

- Ensure that if the store in situated in a regional shopping centre, the total gross rent, comprising base rent, variable outgoings, statutory charges and marketing contribution, does not exceed the benchmark for that category. This information can be obtained from the URBISJHB annual reports on occupancy costs.

Ask yourself the following questions:

Have the premises been surveyed and is there a survey certificate attached to the lease. Since rent and outgoings are measured on a rate per square metre it is vital that the area as shown in the lease is correct.

Is there a cap on the "making good provision" in the lease or will the buyer be faced with a costly removal expense for items like partitions and counters as well as the cost of putting back the premises to its original state? A photo of the premises at the date of handover is useful.

In Victoria, ensure that if there is to be a market review on the exercise of the option in the lease, that there is a provision for the market review to be completed first before you have to exercise your option

Initiating an early lease negotiation

if you are contemplating a sale of the business and you have only 2 years to go on the lease with no further option, it is imperative that you initiate negotiations with your landlord for a new lease as soon as possible. The longer you leave it the more difficult it will be to achieve the desired outcome.

The recent amendments to the retail tenancy legislation in some states set out the legal position regarding early lease negotiation and should be used as a technique for the sale of the business. This applies particularly when there is one year to run plus a 5-year option in your lease. If the lease requires a market review on the exercise of the option, it can be executed as early as possible, and the marker review used to do early as the rental for the start of the option period.

A retailer planning retirement has nothing to fear when opening negotiations with a landlord to initiate a new lease. This should be seen as an opportunity to reset the level of occupancy cost for several years to come.

What about business owners who have given personal guarantees on a lease?

The giving of a personal guarantee on the lease by the directors or shareholders of a tenant in a retail business has become standard practice. But what then happens if the guarantor wishes to retire?

In practice, most landlords will accept the removal of a guarantor on a lease where the owner is retiring, and the business is to be continued by the owner's children.

It is essential that the process is handled formally by the tenant's solicitor acting on behalf of the family. The full details of your exit must be outlined as well as the way the family business will continue to be managed. It must be made clear that the children will replace the father as the guarantor on the lease. It is essential that the solicitor makes clear that this change will not affect the landlord's security on the lease.

Using the lease to have a tax effective and financially equitable disssolution of a partnership

In some instances, the partners in a business, whether it's in a strip centre or stand-alone property, have bought the real estate on which the business is operating. In some cases, the partners have been paying a predetermined rental to the company owning the real estate.

Where one partner intends to take over the business and the other wants to acquire the real estate as his or her "superannuation", the structuring of the lease for the business to continue can be tax effective. It can also allow each partner to meet their own individual goals and objectives.

CHAPTER 26

Capital Gains Tax Concessions Available to Small Businesses on the Sale of a Business

As with all business matters the more you understand, the better your situation while operating your business and later when leaving it. Capital gains tax concerns are a complex area but worth your attention even before consulting your tax adviser.

It is essential that you obtain tax advice in respect of any capital gains tax that may arise on the sale of your business. The following is a guide for discussion with your tax adviser.

What is the small business retirement exemption?

The small business retirement exemption allows qualifying taxpayers to make a capital gain of up to $500,000 without paying any GST, if the relevant requirements are met. Your tax adviser will advise you of the details of the formula and how to apply it to your business.

CHAPTER 27

What Will a Buyer Be Looking at in the Lease When Carrying Out a "Due Dilligence" on the Purchase of the Business?

In arriving at the final selling price of your business, it would be prudent for a potential buyer to carry out a proper due diligence on the lease or leases underpinning the purchase of the business.

There may well be several provisions contained in the lease which may have to be taken into account in the final purchase price. these include:

- Whether the lease provides for a refit of the premises at the end of the current lease term. If it does, it may entail the purchaser having to spend $100000 to $1500000 of his own funds within a short time of taking over the business. This may mean that an appropriate sum of money may have to be deducted from the purchase price.

- Given the flat retail conditions in some centres, the business may have been enjoying a marketing or rental abatement from the landlord of about $2500 per month being credited to the monthly statement. This will mean that the rental paid as per the profit and loss presented is understated.

- Often these abatements will cease on assignment. Such credits should be reinstated and deducted from the profit of the business before applying the "return on investment" percentage.

- Many leases provide for the painting of the store every 3 years. This may well cost up to $5000 for each job. If the date for painting has not yet been reached before the takeover, an equivalent sum should be considered in the purchase price.

- The purchase of a business in a rising rental market where the lease calls for a market review to take place after the date the new buyer has taken over. The purchaser should ask an independent valuer of what the market rent is likely to be.

- A possible substantial increase in the market rental will affect the future profitability of the business and should be taken into account when determining the profitability on which the ROI will be calculated.

- Some leases stipulate that on assignment of the lease, this may trigger an automatic market review. You need to ensure that if this is the case you have a valuer confirming what the rent is likely to be on a market review. This should be considered in the profitability of the business.

- It is important to ascertain the "vintage" of the lease. If you have an old lease and are currently in the second option period, you could be stuck with all the old provisions of the various state acts, and this could be disadvantageous to the new buyer. It may well be a negotiating point for the buyer to rather negotiate a new lease than live with a "bad" old lease.

- If the business is in a centre which is likely to be refurbished or upgraded shortly, there may be certain outgoings like building maintenance, air conditioning being upgraded, or a new centre owner substantially increasing management costs. All these items will cause an increase in future outgoings costs and need to be taken into account in assessing the real future occupancy costs of the business.

- All leases provide for a make good provision at the end of the lease. If your business has been restructured to suit the needs of your current store, there could be a substantial cost involved in returning the store to its original condition. At the point of hand over, ask for any existing photos in existence at the date of hand over. This will allow the purchaser to ascertain the potential liability at the end of the lease.

CHAPTER 28

Planning for Succession if You Have a Business Partner

The retirement or death of your business partner can be very distressing on a personal level. It can also cause havoc in your business if the necessary business plans and agreements for a smooth and trouble-free hand over are not in place.

One of the best approaches is for the partners to put into place a buy/sell agreement or sometimes known as a "cross purchase contract" that sets into place the legal structure by which ownership is transferred.

Though you may have loved your partner as a friend and trusted him completely, can you be so sure about his wife or children? Too many disputes on partnership succession finish up in the courts and involve all parties with substantial legal fees.

It is advisable that a complete business succession partnership plan be drawn up by a competent accountant, supported by solid legal advice where necessary. This may cost a few thousand dollars but it could be the best investment of your life. It will give all parties peace of mind and avoid the conflict and cost that can occur on the departure of a partner.

What should be contained in a buy/sell agreement

- It should cover all situations of possible departure including retirement, death, bankruptcy of a partner, insanity and criminal conviction.

- It must be drawn up in line with the rules that govern the partnership such as the partnership agreement or articles of association, if a company.

- It must be flexible enough to cover the entry of new partners and exit of existing partners.

- It must be unambiguous and easily understood by all parties.

- It must clearly set out the precise chain of events that is to take place to facilitate the departure of a partner and the transfer or sale of the business to the remaining partners or to third parties.

- It must include a timetable to bring effect to the transfer.

- It should also recognize specific periods of mourning as per the religious denominations of the partners.

- It must address the concerns of capital gains tax, stamp duty and other tax considerations. This part of the agreement should be constantly amended as tax legislation changes.

- It must recognize the problem of funding to pay out a partner or his estate and this may include the taking out of life policies and or setting up of annuities to meet the needs of the remaining or surviving partners.

How best to approach and implement the structure of the buy sell agreement

Although solicitors and accountants may advise different approaches, the form of the agreement you follow depends on your relationship with your partner. It may include creating mutual wills or conditional contracts of purchase. From my experience the agreement that seems to work best is the "options basis"

This works in the following way:

- Each partner grants the other an option to purchase each other's interest in the business on the occurrence of an event as contained in the agreement. These options are both a *put* and a *call* option.

- The options are worded so that the amount of the interest has been predetermined at a fixed price, or market price established by a recognized broker acceptable to both parties.

- The option must also bind the executor of each partner's estate. (At present a transfer at a market price may not be subject to stamp duty but that should be checked with your legal adviser in each state).

- The option should be personal to each partner and until such time as the option is formally exercised, each partner retains his full interest in the partnership.

- Funding of the buy-out as indicated above may be by way of a term life policy on each partner's life or a form of annuity

Planning to bring a junior partner into your business

Most exit strategies are usually put in place several years prior to the voluntary departure of an owner. Thus, if you feel that you would like to have that "trial run" of what it's like to play golf on one or two days a week, do not rush out and sell but consider the option of possibly taking on a junior partner.

However, the following considerations need to be considered:

- Nobody likes to have a minority interest in a business and in order to entice a good junior partner you may have to offer an interest of
- 20% – 25% with the option to buy out the balance within 5 years. .All details of succession need to be fully documented, as indicated previously with a proper buy and sell agreement.
- A junior partner may inject into the business a new degree of enthusiasm, which may enhance the business and its eventual value on a sell out.
- Remember a junior partner, like the owner, is looking at several considerations with regard to buying the junior partnership. Some of these will include:-

  1. Not being locked into a minority position with small equity and little management input without the opportunity to increase equity in the future.
  2. Whether he will be able to get along with the senior partner and they will work well together.

3. The junior partner will view it as an opportunity not otherwise available whilst the owner gets a "ready buyer" for the business. Thus it can prove to be a "win-win" situation for both parties.

CHAPTER 29

Selling the Business Outright

As you approach retirement you may arrive at the decision that you wish to sell the business.

We will now look at the actual process of selling your business, under the following topic headings: -

- Planning an exit strategy from the business to achieve a successful outcome, including key issues that will be addressed by the purchaser and strategies to be avoided that will hold up the final sale.
- Appointing and managing a broker during the selling process.
- Determining the worth of the business and the return on investment a potential buyer will be willing to pay.
- Working with a broker to determine the most effective break up of the final selling price, between stock, fixtures, fittings and goodwill.
- Working with a broker to create a good marketing document that displays the business in the best possible light to a potential buyer.
- Minimizing capital gains tax from the sale of the business.
- Preparing the business for sale, including putting stock in order and bringing up to date fixtures and fittings schedules.

PLANNING THE EXIT STRATEGY

To conclude a successful sale of your business, always put yourself in the place of the buyer and try to look at things from his perspective. Think like a buyer and not a seller.

What issues are important to the buyer?

A potential buyer will always consider the risk facing your business at present. Therefore, if for any reason your business is at risk you need to ask yourself the following:

- Do your customers have a relationship with you and not your company?
- Is your supply chain held together with handshakes and "gentlemen's agreements" and not contracts?
- Are you are the only person who knows how every bit of the business works?
- Does your key staff only stay out of loyalty to you?
- Is your Intellectual property in your head?
- Are you using your personal assets as security for your business?
- Do you have contingency plans or a disaster recovery plan?

> *Unless your business can run without you, a new buyer may only pay for what the business is worth. You may need to negotiate to stay on for a defined period. To get the best price you may have to wait on the market. You do not want to sell at the bottom of the market.*

The following are the key issues that most purchasers of a business will want to address.

- Is the price reasonable?
- What is the key "deal breakers" from the buyer's point of view, which will make or break the deal?
- Is the acquisition properly structured?
- What are the sustainable levels of profit and cash flow for the shop?
- If he owns another shop what additional benefits will the acquisition mean for both businesses?
- What are the taxation implications of the acquisition?
- What is the true value of the assets?
- Does the business have proper systems and controls and have the figures been properly audited?
- What are the working capital requirements of the business? If he needs to up-size and put in more stock, will he get assistance from my suppliers?
- How much more capital is needed for fixed assets like a new refit of the premises that may be required under the lease?
- Is there an implementation strategy to ensure that the business operates as planned from day one of the acquisition?

From your point of view as the seller

Making a snap decision that it's time to sell is not very prudent.

If you cannot meet the needs of a buyer as set out above, you will not be able to sell your business to its full value and potential.

Remember that it is critical for the business to show potential to a future buyer so that he will be willing to pay you goodwill.

The key ingredients for a planned exit strategy

- Planning for your exit should be initiated at least 3 to 5 years prior to you exiting the business.

- Invest in proper financial controls and up to date point of sale cash registers capable of analysing sales and gross profits on each item sold by department or product group.

- Have your books audited and have a full set of audited results prepared by a qualified firm of auditors.

- Prepare a budget and a 5-year business plan to be updated annually for the next 5 years.

- Set up a proper open to buy planning system. In this way you can control your purchases to ensure that markdowns are kept to a minimum and gross profits do not fluctuate widely.

- Take a full inventory of your fixtures and fittings with their cost price and a written down value. Your tax returns will be a useful place to ascertain dates of purchase of these fixed assets and their original cost price.

- Enter the inventory into a fixed assets register to be kept until the sale of the business or as you acquire new assets.

- As indicated earlier, ensure that your lease is in order and has several years to run, or contains unconditional options which can be exercised by the new purchaser.

- To enhance the value of the business, it may be worthwhile becoming a member of a marketing group.

- If there are plans to re-route a road near your business or a possible relocation of your store in a shopping centre, make certain that you are aware of all the facts. Don't wait for the purchaser to tell you about it during negotiations. Your local council offices may be very helpful in this regard.

- Finally, contact a broker recommended to you by another retailer satisfied with their sale of their business and the price obtained.

Appointing a broker and managing the broker during the selling process

When you are confident that the business is ready for sale, set the "bush telegraph" into operation by telling your colleagues that your business may be for sale, if you receive the right offer.

The moment you decide to sell your shop you are faced with 2 options: -

1. Do I try to conclude the sale myself and save the commission on the sale

OR

2. Do I contact a broker and let him do the job for me and pay the commission.

From my experience, I find that brokers are professionals at their job of selling a business. The commission that you pay them will be more than covered in the price you receive. A broker will be able to sort out the genuine buyers from the rest.

There are several steps that ought to be taken when dealing with a broker so that the broker carries out the sale according to your wishes.

These include the following:

- Determining the type of broker you want to deal with, meeting with a number of brokers, and selecting one you feel most comfortable with before making the appointment.
- Prior to the appointment, it is wise to prepare a document of sale which can be used by the broker as part of the selling process.

This document should include the following:

◊ The selling price that you believe the shoe shop is worth.
◊ Your means of allocating the price between stock, fixtures and fittings and goodwill.
◊ An available layout of the store together with a location plan.
◊ A copy of the lease and if you are in the process of negotiations, copies of the latest correspondence with the landlord.
◊ A copy of the audited accounts of the shop for the past 3 years.
◊ A trend analysis showing growth patterns of sales and profits over the last 3 years in order to demonstrate to a potential buyer a strong profitable business.
◊ Some colour photos of the premises from both outside and inside.

Use your accountant or a business adviser to critically analyse and assess your information and financial data used in support of your valuation.

- Having decided on which form of broker you wish to use, take the document with your views about the sale to the broker for initial discussion.

- Discuss the document in detail with the broker. Take into consideration his analysis of the market and his assessment of your business potential. You will need to take a flexible approach and be prepared to amend your expectations on the selling price. No doubt you will be able to assess whether the broker is an expert in the area.

- It is important not to set your expectations too high. Often the initial discussion can be very distressing. No store owner is happy to hear that their life's work is not worth as much as they thought it was.

- Once you have the broker's commitment to the sale, confirm his appointment in writing. Clarify whether he is hired exclusively or for a period of months.

- Later, ensure that any potential buyers that the broker introduces to you are prepared to make an offer in your price range.

- Once the deal is concluded ensure that the broker is paid his commission in full.

CHAPTER 30

Valuation of the Business

It is accepted in the industry that a retail business is usually valued on a return-on-investment basis.

This method is determined by the following procedures: -

- Taking the adjusted net profit of the business as per the audited accounts
- Deducting an appropriate salary for the Owner/Managers
- The resulting figure is called the return on investment or R.O.I.
- The R.O.I is now multiplied by 100 and divided by the required return.
- This now gives us the total purchase price of the business.

Example:

If after your accountant has made the appropriate adjustments to net profit before tax by deducting extraneous income and adding back deductions (that would not apply to the new business), you have a net profit before tax of $200000.

The business is one with potential in a good location, with a good lease in place and a low risk attached to it and a return of 18% is considered appropriate.

The manager or owner of the business earns a salary of $50000.

Then the ROI will be
$$200000 - 50000$$
$$= 150000$$

The value of the business will be
$$\frac{150000 \times 100}{18}$$
$$= \$833333$$

Thus, on an investment of $833333 the new buyer will receive a return of 18% on his investment

The professionalism of the broker

The crucial element is to know what percentage returns to apply. And here is where the professionalism of the broker comes into play.

In times of high interest rates up to 25% ROI can be anticipated. In a low interest market as at present, 15% may be sufficient, considering a risk factor over the current interest rates.

The question people often ask a broker or adviser is, how do I assess the future potential of the business?

In assessing potential there are several elements to be considered such as:

- The sales growth of the business over the past 3 to 5 years.
- The quality of the competition in the area or shopping centre.
- The traffic flow movements to the shopping centre over the past 3 years.
- The population increases and developments in the area.

Once you have established the purchase of the business, you now have to break up this price into its three components namely.

- Stock
- Value of Fixtures and Fittings
- Goodwill

A. Valuation of stock

The valuation of stock usually refers to the valuation on the day of sale.

However, the valuation can also be fairly accurately calculated from the retailers own audited profit and loss account.

The valuation is calculated by taking the average of the opening and closing stocks as shown in the previous accounts.

Example:

Stock at the Start of the year	=	$100500
Closing Stock For Year	=	$110700
		$211200

$211200 divided by 2	=	$105600 Average
Rounded off to		$106000

B. Valuation of fixtures and fittings

There are two basic methods of arriving at the value of the fixtures and fittings:

Estimating the written down value of the assets as per the fixed asset register or as per the retailers' tax file forming a support schedule to the tax return for the business.

OR

Estimating the market value of fixtures and fittings.

The advantage from the seller's point of view, of using the written down value, is that it results in no capital gains tax being payable on the difference between the written down value and the market value.

The assets may be worth a lot more than their written down value. This method may be preferable as it more accurately reflects what a willing buyer would pay in a sale of an ongoing business.

In addition, the higher the value of the fixtures and fittings, the more the seller will be able to claim as a reduction for taxation (in respect of depreciation on such higher assets.)

No stamp duty is payable on the fixtures and fittings component of the sale, so this is a further incentive to value fixtures and fittings at "best" market value.

C. Goodwill

The value of the stock, plus the agreed value of the fixtures and fittings subtracted from the total price as assessed above, gives the goodwill component of the price.

GST

If the business is sold as a going concern it will not attract GST. However, if the taxation office determines that the sale of the business was not a genuine sale "of a going concern", the sale of the property will be liable for GST.

If the vendor assumes that the sale is a going concern, but the tax office rules that it is not, the vendor will be left bearing the cost of the GST. This may or may not be later recoverable from the buyer. It is advisable to check this point with your tax adviser.

It is worth considering that in order to obtain the GST exemption, the tax office has ruled in advance that a vendor can supply leased premises as part of the sale of the business as a going concern, by either assigning the existing lease or arranging for the lessor to grant a new lease before the completion date. Similar treatment will also apply to franchise agreements.

The tax office has relaxed its views regarding the transfer of employees as a requirement for a going concern to be actually transferred. However, if "key employees" have skills or knowledge that are essential to the continued operation of the going concern, that knowledge or skill, must be transferred. The new employer is not required to employ the key staff members.

Once again check these points with your tax adviser.

CHAPTER 31

Spending and Investing Your Money

Congratulations! You have now sold your business and now you have the pleasant task of deciding what you are going to do with the money.

Planning your finances for retirement is essential. If done properly and with care, you can be assured of a retirement free from financial worry.

Building a successful financial plan involves assessing the funds you have now, deciding on your needs for the future and how long your money needs to last.

I suggest that you appoint a financial adviser. This is often not as easy as it seems.

In selecting an adviser, the following criteria should be met: -

- The adviser must be a person who will continue to take care of you long after your investments have been placed.
- He must be a licensed dealer with the Australian Securities Commission.

- Some advisers may only have a licence restricted to dealing only in certain investments or securities. Ask your adviser if his license has any restrictions.

- Your adviser should be qualified and involved in ongoing training to ensure that he is abreast of the latest legislation and investment strategies.

- Make sure that your adviser has the resources and research facilities to keep abreast of happenings in the investment market and the economy, as well as changes in taxation and financial legislation.

- Be certain that your adviser agrees to send you regular reports and financial statements and that he will keep in contact with you if any changes or opportunities arise that may affect your financial position.

Paying your adviser

Before you ask an adviser to develop a financial plan for you, ascertain how he will be paid for this and determine the payment options available to you.

Financial advisers are usually paid in the following ways: -

- The whole question of financial advisor fees has been amended by the government and you need to be fully familiar with the new regulations before you discuss the question of fees with your adviser.

- By way of a commission when they place your investment with an investment company. The commission is paid to the adviser by the investment company out of the entry fee that the investment company deducts when you invest. The commission is not usually charged as an extra cost to you.

- If you were to approach the investment company directly without using your adviser, you would still be charged the same entrance fee with no commission payable. Therefore, it is no cheaper to go directly to the company or via the adviser.

- The adviser may charge you on a fixed sliding scale depending on how much you invest and how much time he has taken to work with you. Often an adviser charging a fee will refund to you any commission received from the investment company.

Your plan

Having selected the appropriate investment advisor and concluded your first meeting to discuss your financial position and goals for the future, request a written financial plan for review by yourself and your family.

The plan prepared by the adviser should contain at least the following criteria:

- That all recommendations should be clearly explained and backed up with current research.

- If the investments include the placing of your funds in a managed fund, this should be supported by details of the investment managers as well as a history of their past performance.

- You should be confident that his recommendations offer you the right level of security and that you will not be putting your money in risky investments, especially in view of the current financial climate.

- The plan includes an estimate of the likely returns that your investment will achieve and when income payments will be received.
- It should outline an explanation of how you can gain access to your funds in an emergency.
- There should be an explanation on how your investments will affect your pension or other government entitlements.
- There must be a clear statement of the cost of implementing the plan and how and when you will have to pay the required amounts.
- There should be a disclosure statement showing any commissions that your adviser will receive.
- In essence, the plan should cover all issues that are important to you and your financial future

HAVE A HAPPY AND ENJOYABLE RETIREMENT!

www.ingramcontent.com/pod-product-compliance
Lightning Source LLC
Chambersburg PA
CBHW071659200326
41519CB00012BA/2572